Wrapped in Joy

Franciscan Poor Clare Sisters
Share Special Stories

Sister Katherine, O.S.C.

Welcome by Murray Bodo, O.F.M.

DWH Publishing
Dallas, Texas

Editors: Sister Katherine, O.S.C., Sister Charlene Toups, O.S.C., Debra Hampton
Book Designer: Darcy B. Hecht
Page Layout: Darcy B. Hecht
Cover Designer: Kevin Fremder
Cover Illustration: Sister Clare Ellen Wittman, O.S.C.

DWH Publishing
9707 Galway Drive
Dallas, Texas 75218
Distributed by Park Press
Waite Park, Minn.

Table of Contents

4

PART 4: *From Glory to Glory* **203**
Sisters who served Our Lord in an active order
and then transferred to the Poor Clares.

Dedication

To our God who planted the seed and opened all the doors and windows...

To Saint Clare for her "yes" to God and for giving us all such a beautiful example of obedience, holiness, gentleness and love...

To the Poor Clare Sisters who have gone before us...

To those who are living the life at this time in history...

To you, the next Poor Clare Sisters, whom God is calling to help keep our vision alive...

To all of you who have loved, prayed for and helped us over the years...

To those of you who might not know either Saint Clare or any of her sisters, yet you're reading *Wrapped in Joy*....

This book is dedicated to you!

WELCOME to the world of stories. We are our stories, and stories are not just a chronology of what happened. Stories are why things happened, those surprising interventions of God, those seemingly coincidental meetings, those decisions we never thought would bring us here to the place where we are now.

From the very beginning Franciscan Spirituality has much to do with stories: the stories of Francis and Clare, the stories they told and wrote down of God's marvelous Providence and surprising intervention in their lives. So that instead of a methodology of spiritual growth, Franciscans have stories, parables, like the story of "Perfect Joy," that encapsulates (like the parables of Christ Himself) the essence of what it means to follow in the footsteps of Christ.

In the story of "Perfect Joy," Francis and Leo are on the road, and Francis presents several scenarios of the brothers' great accomplishments and tells Brother Leo that none of this success and spiritual achievement is perfect joy. No, he says, this is perfect joy: When we arrive at St. Mary of the Angels, the brother porter does not recognize us and drives us away. And we keep coming back and insisting we are who we say we are, but he doesn't believe us and comes out at last with a club and beats us and heaps verbal abuse on us. If when this happens, we bear it peacefully for the love of Jesus Christ, then that is perfect joy.

The Franciscan story from Francis and Clare till now in the 21st Century is filled with stories like "Perfect Joy" and other stories like those in these pages, lovingly gathered: stories of women who have responded to God's call and entered the monastery of St. Clare of Assisi, the first woman Franciscan. Here are stories of lives diverse in age, experience, personality and background. And yet God's Providence has brought them together in monasteries across America and throughout the world. What makes them cohere? What is the core story that their stories all partake of? It is the story of Christ, surely, but more specifically it is the story of a way of extending Christ's story which St. Clare lived and handed down to her sisters.

It is the story of a medieval woman, Clare, the daughter of the Knight Favarone and his noble wife Ortolana. It is the story of a woman who already as a young girl was given to prayer and

almsgiving. And then she hears St. Francis
preach and she hears in his words the same
desire for God that she is already experiencing,
the same conviction that God is revealed everywhere, even (and perhaps especially) in the poor
and the rejected, the marginal people who live
outside the walls of Francis' and Clare's town of
Assisi. God is even in and with the lepers.

In the end she follows Francis despite the
opposition of her family and friends; and with a
friend and her sister, Clare founds the first
monastery of Franciscan women in the little
church of San Damiano outside the walls of
Assisi. It is the first church restored by St.
Francis, the church where his own vocation
began when he heard a voice from the crucifix
say to him, "Francis, go and repair my house
which, as you see, is falling into ruin."

It is the place of Francis' prophecy recorded
by St. Clare in her Testament: "Immediately
after his conversion and before St. Francis had
any brothers or companions, he spent his time
repairing the church of San Damiano. There he
received that vision of the Lord which filled him
with heavenly consolation; there he made his
final decision to leave the world, and there in a

transport of joy and enlightened by the Holy Spirit, he prophesied something about us which the Lord later fulfilled.

"He climbed the wall of the church and cried out in French to some poor people standing around, 'Come and help me build this monastery of San Damiano because in a short time some ladies are going to live here whose holy lives will bring glory to our Heavenly Father throughout the whole Church.'"

There at San Damiano Clare lives out her life in contemplation of the Crucified Christ, in serving the needs of her sisters, and in sharing with her sisters a life of radical Gospel poverty.

And the monastery grows and prospers, and other monasteries are founded, and they still are being founded today. Women keep coming to contemplate Christ Crucified, to learn love by serving one another, to live a poor life as witnesses of the poverty of God as revealed in Jesus Christ.

These are their stories: stories of the richness of true poverty, of the goodness of God, of the ongoing call to conversion, of the special call to follow Christ as a virgin living with other women a life of contemplation and charity, and of the joy that such a life brings.

May your hearts be touched, as mine was, as you read these stories of the wonder of God's call and the myriad responses of those who hear and say, "Yes!"

Fr. Murray Bodo, O.F.M.
Cincinnati, Ohio

The Story Of Clare And Her Form of Life

In 2003-2004 Franciscans throughout the world celebrate two events: the 750th anniversary of the approval by Pope Innocent IV of "the form of life of the Order of the Poor Sisters that Blessed Francis established," and the death of Clare of Assisi that occurred shortly after she received the Pope's approval for this form of life. This book, *Wrapped in Joy*, holds the stories of women who have been called to live this form of life known in our times as the Rule of Clare.

Francis of Assisi is well known throughout the world and loved by persons of all faiths. Clare was his friend and collaborator, establishing a community for women who wanted to follow Jesus Christ with whole-hearted commitment. One of Clare's favorite metaphors for following Jesus was "to walk in His footprints."

Clare followed in the footprints of Jesus, and her prints were not swept away in the sands of time. We see the footprints of Clare made by all of her daughters who have both lived and rediscovered her Rule and walked her path throughout the centuries in every culture, climate and condition including our own time. Let us follow these footprints, walking backward to the 13th century and the beginning of this form of life.

In ancient Israel from time to time the Book of the Covenant, the account of the pact between God and his people, had to be rediscovered anew. After tears and shouts of joy, the people of Israel would recommit themselves to God. It was like that in the time of Francis and Clare. The 13th century was a time of renewal in the Church and society. Lateran Council IV, not unlike our own Vatican Council II, was a great Church assembly that had gathered to renew the Christian people in every aspect of their lives, but especially to hold up to the people the Liturgy. In the Liturgy, the prayer of the Church, the Hebrew and Christian Scriptures are proclaimed, the Word of God is interpreted by effective preaching and the holy Sacrament of the Eucharist is celebrated.

It was in this climate of renewal in the 13th century that Francis and Clare gathered with many brothers and sisters to live the Christian gospel anew. The first Franciscans experienced covenant renewal in a familial relation to Christ and gospel poverty.

Both Francis and Clare with their brothers and sisters formulated rules to live this covenant relation. What is the Franciscan Rule, and in particular, the form of life of the Poor Sisters of St. Clare? The Clarian form of life can best be seen in the light of the "Law" as it is understood in ancient Israel and in the letters of St. Paul, the great apostle of Christ. The Law in Israel and according to Paul is

God's expression of the divine order and goodness in all created reality, in all persons and everything that exists. The Law is a tutor for humankind to see and reflect the image of God stamped in creation. Similarly the Franciscan Rules — that is, the rules professed by the various branches of the Franciscan Family — invite us to a way of being and behaving in God's loving company, naming and expressing the goodness, truth and beauty of life in God and the interdependence of all created reality.

Just as the Israelites formulated many minor rules to protect the Law, the great covenant with God, Clare, in her Rule, gives specific instructions how to live so as to realize God's goodness, truth and beauty in one's life and in the community. The most important of all the particular regulations in Clare's Rule affirming this covenant with God is the invitation to live without anything of one's own, both individually and communally. Poverty in material possessions as well as in the ordering of one's days is the personal and communal practice that gives authenticity and outward expression of the inner commitment of one's mind, heart and soul in God. Everything comes from God, the giver of life and all that is good. Franciscans are urged to appreciate everything and to cling to nothing.

In ancient Israel, the enthusiasm for the Covenant with God waxed and waned. So too has it been with the followers of Clare down through the centuries. The Rule of Clare held up a difficult challenge, particularly in regard to poverty. Often the nuns would be asked by the Church to follow a modified version of the Rule of Clare, such as the one authored by Pope Urban IV in 1263, ten years after the death of Clare. It was called the Urbanist Rule and in contrast to the Rule of Clare it permitted communal ownership of property and fixed revenues. Clare's Rule was approved in 1253 for her Sisters at San Damiano, living outside the city of Assisi. Following the death of Clare the community left their poor little monastery to move inside the walls of Assisi and to the newly built monastery of St. Clare. In 1284 the community accepted the Urbanist Rule as their guide.

Thus, down through the centuries, the Rule of Clare was set aside and then would, like the Covenant of old, have to be rediscovered, thereby generating a renewal among women wanting to follow the Franciscan path anew. This happened in various countries. Colette of Corbie (1381-1447), for example, was a reformer of both the Sisters of St. Clare and the Franciscan Friars. She reformed or founded monasteries in France, Vevey in Switzerland and Heidelberg in Germany. Her reform movement continues to flourish to the present day. In Italy the reform was led by Catherine of Bologna (1413-1463), Camilla Battista Varani (1458-1524) and Veronica Giuliani (1660-1727). Caritas Pirckheimer (1467-1532) was a leader in the reform during the Protestant suppression of religious orders in Germany.

Closer to our own times, Maddalena Bentivoglio (1834-1905) from the Poor Clare Monastery of San Lorenzo Panisperna, Rome, arrived in New York in 1875. She carried a mandate from Pope Pius IX to begin a Poor Clare foundation not of the Colettine form of Clarian life but of the more primitive observance, that is the Rule of St. Clare, in the United States. The story of this foundress is one of courage in the face of incredible obstacles, faith and devotion before humiliation and betrayal. From this beginning at the end of the 19th century stem twenty-four monasteries in the United States and six overseas foundations.

As the Clares of today relate their vocation stories they are united with their Sisters through the centuries, all of whom have found their life commitment in following in the footprints of Jesus after the manner of Francis and Clare of Assisi.

Sister Beth Lynn, O.S.C.
Minneapolis, Minnesota

Introduction

Vocation

One of the many interesting aspects of vocation is that each call or vocation develops in a unique way which is quite specific to that individual. Yet, at the same time, there are certain fundamental factors or elements present in that vocation which indicate a call into this religious family, this particular charism. As a result, when we come to read a collection of vocation histories like this one, we are struck by the amazing variety of the stories, but also by an indefinable Something that is shared by them all. Part of the task of discerning vocations, of course, lies in teasing out those common elements and recognizing in them the outlines of the Poor Clare, the Benedictines, the apostolic Franciscan and so on. In this book, we have unmistakably Poor Clare stories. Insert a Jesuit story and it would instantly be spotted!

What is vocation?

Francis and Clare understood clearly that they had been called by the grace of the Father. It was all gift from the Most High Heavenly Father for His own purposes. This call came to them through the Holy Spirit. It was a call to follow in the footprints of Jesus Christ, the Son of God made man.

"No one showed me what I should do, but the Lord himself told me" said Francis in his Testament not long before his death. Clare, on her part, said: "the Most High heavenly Father deigned by his grace to enlighten my heart."

Each of them responded in a unique way to this: Francis as a contemplative apostle, Clare as an apostolic contemplative. Each of them understood that the invitation of the Crucifix in San Damiano: "Repair my church," was a command/invitation that gave shape to their basic vocation. This is the call, too, of all those today who come, however vaguely, under the extremely broad Franciscan umbrella.

What was this enlightenment of the heart of which Clare speaks? Notice it was the heart which was enlightened, excellent though her head was. We remember Francis' prayer: enlighten the darkness of my heart. By the grace of God, Clare's heart was enlightened to do penance, that is, to change her way of life, so that she followed the poor Christ, in humility, in poverty and in simplicity. These were not pious words, but a passionately held conviction of the call to minoritas which might be translated by lesserness, a sharing in the redemptive self-emptying of Christ. It was, especially for Clare the aristocrat, a call to downward mobility. She lived this faithfully and taught others to live it. As a result, we can now read her life as an instruction for us and can begin to discern in her story the outlines of the charism she held in trust from God. It is this charism, given to her by the Spirit, which she faithfully handed on to those who came after her — that is, to us today. From our vantage point of nearly 800 years, we can see that our fidelity has had good years and not so good years, though it has never been lost altogether, by the grace of God.

Perhaps the most powerful message Clare gives us is in the wonderful Chapter Eight of her Rule. In this chapter, she makes it clear that she knows she and her sisters have been called to something quite new.

"This is that height of most high poverty which has established you, my dearest sisters, heiresses and queens of the Kingdom of heaven, which has made you poor in things, sublime in virtue. Let her (poverty) be your portion, let her be the one who will lead you into the land of the living. Clinging wholly to her, dearest sisters, for the name of our Lord Jesus Christ and his most holy Mother, do not wish to have anything else under heaven, ever." (Rule of Clare 8: 4-5)

Such an attitude was a long way from that of monastic life of her time. In fact, this whole section of Clare's Rule, Chapters 6-10, can be read as a sustained reflection on *sine proprio*, on having nothing of one's own, of being free from possessiveness and the desire for property. This was not an obsessive nihilism. All Clare's thinking and living were fundamentally relational. The source for her thinking, the model for her understanding and living, was the generous flow of life and being within the Trinity itself. "How wonderful it is," said Francis, "that there are those who want nothing but Your own Most glorious Self." Clare sought to imitate this generous flow of life and love. She was certainly pre-eminent among those who wanted nothing but 'Your own most glorious Self.' Surely, today too, this lies at the heart of the gift given by the Spirit through her to the Church. At its very best, Poor Clare life is a generous sharing in the total self-giving of the Trinity. It is a life in which even the self is not owned but shared, a life in which relationships are the medium, the way, through which the self flows outward. Relationships are learned from the Primary Relater, God, and without this turning to others, this apostolic openness, the contemplative Poor Clare life can become sterile indeed. Paradoxically, the outward sign of this inward grace is the joyous presence of Most High Poverty, the hallmark of self-giving. The presence of that lady, the Lady Poverty, indicates that the essential characteristics, the marks of Franciscanism, are present. Every Christian is called to enter into the dynamism of the Trinity. Every Franciscan is called, in a particular way, to enter into a profound union with the humanity of Jesus, particularly in his self-emptying and in His passion. Every Poor Clare is called to cleave with all her heart to him whom the sun and moon adore.

As a poor virgin, embrace the poor Christ.

How hard this is to do in a materialistic age — or so we might think. Yet has it ever been easy? Has it ever even been possible? Is the whole enterprise not continuing today as it began for Clare, solely by the gracious calling of the Most High heavenly Father? It demands no special gifts of those who receive that call, though it might demand that the gifts be constellated in a special way. It is possible that Poor Clares have a particular psychic, spiritual and moral profile, though Poor Clares are in fact so varied that this could equally well not be true! Perhaps the reader of these stories will discover whether this be true or not.

Can we venture to draw a profile for the charism given to Clare of Assisi in 1212? This could be important for discernment of vocations, especially if we believe that this charism is still alive and active, still cutting like a sharp two-edged sword. I think we can have a try even if only to suggest that at its best, it is characterized by:

- freedom
- generosity in love
- external poverty reflecting the absence of inner possessiveness
- a growing readiness, especially as life moves on and, at the same time, a growing ability to enter into the Passion of Christ

At its worst, might the opposites be present: an imprisoned soul, unloving, possessive and even greedy for the prop of material things, a heart closed to the pain of the Passion? This is a picture one would hope never to see.

All the positive qualities converge, so to speak, in the mirror of Christ Himself to which we return again and again. This was Clare's advice to us: "Place your mind before the mirror of eternity." There we recover that perspective which gives us joy instead of distress, because Christ is a hero who has won through his ordeal most gloriously and we are all free in consequence! It is he who will lead us all onward until we come into his wine cellar and at this point in our pilgrimage, we do not really know what that will mean. It is a universal call, not just for Poor Clares; but perhaps what is specific to Poor Clares is the task of keeping the path clear and well-trodden so that the people of God can find their way more easily. "I think of you," said Clare to Agnes of Prague, "as of one who lifts up from beneath those failing members of Christ's body" — that is a fairly literal translation, but there is something very beautiful about that lifting up from beneath, that lifting up from the privileged position of lesserness.

Sister Frances Teresa, O.S.C.
Sussex, England

"Bless the Lord, my soul!
Lord God, how great you are,
clothed in majesty and glory,
wrapped in light as in a robe!"

Psalm 104:2

"I Heard the Voice of Jesus Say..."

Sisters share how they heard Jesus speak in the quiet of their hearts.

The Path of Freedom
(A Scripture-Based Reflection)

Father, my Father, I thank you for the wonder of my being. Before the mountains or the world were brought forth, O Lord, you are. You, who are love, knew me from the beginning, for all things are of your making. When the time was right, you breathed forth your Spirit and brought me into being; created me that I might come to know you and love you and sing the praises of your glory forever. It was you who knit me together in my mother's womb. A sinner was I conceived but you were with me from the beginning.

In your wisdom you placed me in a family that was poor and simple, not in the least sophisticated. We lived on a quiet farmland in the midst of the beauty of the Canadian prairie: the still mornings, the glorious sunsets, the exquisitely fragile beauty of wild crocuses, the power of thunder, the joy of snow; with all these and more you enticed me and I was enticed, Lord. My soul knew that you were there and that you were far beyond my understanding.

In your tender compassion, you parted the veil one summer afternoon, when I was twelve or so. You drew me to an open field, away from all the buildings and allowed me to hear and to feel your silence, your great and terrible silence. From within me there arose a song, high and pure, and I lifted it to the sky for a long time. In your kindness, you let me taste the joy of your love. How blessed you are Lord, great and beyond compare. You didn't have to do that, but you did, and because of that afternoon I came to know, many years later, what it was that you wanted of me.

You had me taught by dedicated educators and a natural bent for learning was nourished and fostered. Some of my teachers were religious and these consecrated women were real examples of virtue for me. In their company, I came to love goodness and because of their patient gentleness, handicaps were not obstacles but challenges to be met. Many years were to elapse before I knew the gift they had given me.

I left home in search of freedom. I looked everywhere. And you let me search. I went to hell and back. Following the wrong path, I lived in the wilderness under satan's dominion. But you would not leave my soul among the dead. The Spirit with which you had anointed me made me cry out to you in my worst hour when I thought that all was lost. "Our Father!" was all I could say but I would cry it out with all the strength of my soul.

My mother died during these years of my darkest hour. On the night in which she died I experienced a peace that I had never known before. Deep in my heart there came a certainty that everything was going to be alright. As I hit rock bottom I clung to this hope, the only light I had in the midst of terrifying darkness. Bound by an enslavement worse than any prison, I could do nothing and so you did for me what I could not do myself: you saved me. With your mighty arm and your strong right hand you drew me out of the prison I was in and I returned to live with my Father. "Come," He said, "come quickly."

In your great mercy, my God, you opened the heart of my human father to receive me so that my life might be turned around. When you took him to yourself in death, you placed good people in my path and gave me a stable income and a home to live in. I began to hear the Name of Jesus Christ. Acquaintances encouraged me to get to know Him. One weekend, at a prayer meeting I heard the Word of God and for the first time in my life I cried the tears of repentance. It was the Prologue to the Gospel of John and I couldn't read it often enough. I devoured it. "You know…you could always go to confession," someone said to me. "I could?" I thought to myself, very surprised. But the idea would not go away and I plucked up the courage to do so.

The priest who received me took his priesthood seriously and, with a firm, yet ever so gentle hand set me on the right path. He saved my life. Through him, Father, you set me on a rock and made my footsteps firm. Slowly, very slowly, and painstakingly did he set about renewing my love for you. I learned how to pray. I learned to love and reverence your Mother and the Church. My return to the sacraments was joy beyond description. To have you alive in my soul and to just be near you was all I wanted.

It was then that I met the Poor Clares. It was in meeting them that I knew that they possessed the joy that I wanted. My spiritual director did not encourage me nor discourage me. He waited.

On the feast of St. Angela of Merici, I was awakened by someone calling my name, "Roberta." "I want you to be...", and then there was a long, long pause before it continued, "like a Poor Clare and be an example for all sinners." I turned on the light and looked at the crucifix hanging on the wall at the foot of the bed. "Me?" I said, "Me? Really?" But, oh the joy and the sheer wonder of it!

The road to the monastery door was a long one. There were many obstacles to overcome. With bands of love you drew me to your holy enclosure where you placed me in the care of wise and sensitive formators and directors who never stopped believing in your love for me. With patience and perseverance they claimed your victory over me that I might be able to give myself entirely to you. As the years go by, I come to see that you were with me at every moment of my life, in every place, in every circumstance. Loving me. Saving me. And so all of my life — all of it — is a blessing in Jesus Christ, for you are my God. You were carrying me all the while, as a Father carries his littlest child, all along her journey.

Sister Roberta Marie Lapierre, O.S.C.
Mission, B.C., Canada

"...at San Damiano, Clare cast the anchor of her soul in a secure site. In this little house of penance the virgin Clare enclosed herself for love of her heavenly spouse. Here she imprisoned her body for as long as it would live hiding it from the turmoil of the world. In the hollow of this wall...she gave birth to a gathering of virgins of Christ, founded a holy monastery and began the Order of the Poor Ladies." LegCl 10

The Story Of A Vocation

"Here I am! You called me?" (1 Samuel 3:5)

When did it begin? So difficult to determine when those first yearnings began to be felt. For many years God's voice was so gentle, I did not know it was God; I only knew that I had a desire to be near Him, if only in small ways. When all the schoolchildren gathered in church for Mass, many times my mind was distracted and my focus elsewhere, but always there was a steady warmth — a low, secret delight — to be in the church, near His altar and His tabernacle, even though I could never name the desire.

Why else on those warm spring afternoons would I find myself pedaling back to the church on my bicycle? What had started as an aimless ride around the neighborhood after the homework was done became a regular patrolling of the sidewalks and the parking lot, going over every well-known crack and bump. The bicycle would stop and, leaning it against the wall, I would peer into the locked, vacant church to get a glimpse of the great emptiness inside, somehow lonely, yet so attractive and full of mystery. Of course, no such thoughts ever articulated themselves in my 10-year-old mind; all I knew was that I felt peaceful here, near God's house and always wanted to come back.

As a teenager, I had the opportunity to become more involved in parish activities: I was asked to be a lector and then a few years later to participate in the Youth Mass music group. Life became more full of activity, yet God's voice often would speak to me clearly of a great desire to be His. I most vividly remember the intention offered at the Sunday Mass for vocations. Each time I heard it, I felt as though God were speaking directly to me; it was the beginning of a great certainty deep within myself of my religious call, although it would take many years to fully realize it.

High school and college were even busier times as I prepared myself for my future. The constant question seemed to be: "What do I want to do with my life?" Religious life never seriously entered my mind which was occupied with far more short-term concerns: passing exams, interviewing for jobs. How often we are able to look back on our lives and see the smallness of the world to which we confine ourselves! However, at the time, it was my only world and the only direction that seemed open to me. Having a practical bent, I had majored in business. Even with such a practical degree, I had difficulty finding employment in my native area of Louisiana which was experiencing a recession. After three months of fruitless searching, through a friend I was offered a job in New York City. I felt the Lord's call to adventure, excitement, new discoveries, and off I went!

"Eli said: 'I did not call. Go back and lie down.'"

(1 Samuel 3:5)

Those five years in New York were a very exciting time! The endless diversions and countless young people made it easy to feel alive and in the mainstream of life. Was this, then, where God had called me to stay? As time wore on, a nagging sensation of emptiness began to grow. The glamour and glitter of city life slowly faded, replaced by weariness over the constant stimulation of novelty and a lack of rootedness. I needed to go home. Yet where was home for me?

Believing my restlessness a result of career boredom, I enrolled in business school in North Carolina. Upon graduation two years later, I moved to Kansas City, where I had been offered a job. Finally, it seemed I had found a city with everything I needed: a good job with prospects of advancement, a city with friendly people and a slower pace, and a thriving Catholic community. After a few years, however, I still sensed something missing — a commitment of some sort — and having come close to marriage a few times, I decided when I was 30 to "give a try" to the idea of religious life that had haunted me for so long.

"Speak, Lord, for your servant is listening."

(1 Samuel 3:10)

First I spoke with my pastor who gave me the names of a few religious communities in the area. I contacted the Franciscan Sisters of the Holy Eucharist — an active community — and began what was to be a long friendship. After attending a vocation retreat there, I continued to meet with their vocation director. After only a short time I felt that God was calling me to the contemplative life, although still within the Franciscans. Sister supplied me with a listing of all religious communities in the U.S. and also some advertising material, including the *Vision* magazine and *Your Choice* booklet (the latter is no longer printed). When I opened the *Your Choice* booklet, the first thing I saw was a picture of a sister praying in front of the Crucifix-monument in Langhorne. I cannot explain it, but the instant I saw the picture a flame lit my heart and I knew I wanted to meet those sisters! After a few years' correspondence and visits, finally I received the greatest wish of my heart and I entered! January 25, 1998, the Feast of the Conversion of St. Paul, will always be a very special day for me.

"Yahweh said to Abram, 'leave your country, your family and your father's house, for the land I will show you.'" (Genesis 12:1)

At last I seemed to have found my heart's desire — to give myself to God completely, allowing Him to love the whole world through me. How especially happy were those first few months: my body seemed to be floating, my heart singing with joy all day, every day. Loving God and giving myself to Him completely was so much easier than I thought it would be! Sometimes, thoughts of my family who were so far away would make me sad; however, my joy at my newfound life was always far greater and the sadness would quickly melt away.

Unfortunately, or rather for the long run, fortunately, honeymoons don't last very long. As I became accustomed to life in the monastery, my feelings of great consolation began to fade and my emotions settled at a more normal level. Life was still very good because I knew I was where the Lord wanted me. After so many years of empty searching, the belief that God wanted me here and was working through me to reach others made the life very much worth living.

Various difficulties began to present themselves. The first great challenge was community living. As anyone living in a community will agree to, every single person is very different in her likes, dislikes, personality and upbringing. I seemed to find myself in conflict with a sister, usually a different one every other week! Always the conflicts were small, but they represented a much larger conflict within myself: how to let go of the belief that everyone had to think or act like myself! It is easy to laugh now at those conflicts, but many hurt feelings did occur. Thanks be to God and to St. Clare for the forgiving spirit which St. Clare herself exemplified and which fills her houses! I thank God even for the conflicts for they have allowed me to grow closer to Him and to my sisters and to be more compassionate.

Family issues were another great conflict. Even though I had lived far from them before, I had always been free to visit them whenever I wished. Now my family had to come to me. The distance was a difficulty for them as well as the shyness about visiting a monastery. However, in time everyone became comfortable and, in addition to the occasional visits, there is much communication via email and telephone. I communicate much more frequently and meaningfully with my family now, compared to my premonastic life, when I took them a little more for granted.

Many other difficulties have arisen and disappeared in the five years that I have been a Poor Clare nun. One of the most trying temptations, as many in the spiritual life will tell you, is that of dryness in prayer and the accompanying feeling that God has abandoned us. In hindsight, we know that God never abandons us but only wishes us to seek Him more deeply and, in fact, is always much closer than we could ever imagine. What has sustained me through these sometimes very strong temptations? God's gift of faith, I suppose, and the prayers of all my sisters and of all those who pray for us. By God's grace I am more certain of my vocation after one of these struggles; I am sure that they are truly a great gift.

Well, that is the story of a vocation, short in years so far but long in desire. May the Lord give you, reader, great peace and an open heart to His call for you.

Sister Anne Bartol, O.S.C.
Langhorne, Pennsylvania

"There is our vocation for which...we owe the greatest thanks to Him."
TestCl 3

The Long Journey

On Sunday, January 10, 1988, I entered the Poor Clare Monastery in Evansville, Indiana. It was the feast of Our Lord's Baptism and I was full of joy that I was finally here. I was 52 years old and it had been a long, long journey. I could look back and see many ways that God had called and prepared me.

Two years before that day, I was praying in my apartment in New York City, when suddenly I understood God telling me: "You think you don't have a vocation, but you do." I was surprised and awed at this understanding. It was so clear and strong that I had no doubt that it was God's "voice." I answered that I was too old and that my mother needed me too much. God replied that my age didn't matter and that He would take care of my mother.

My vocation started long before that. When I was 13 years old and still an Episcopalian, I read a biography of St. Francis. I never forgot the attraction I felt after reading that book to both St. Francis and St. Clare. I even felt drawn to the monastic life.

When I was 14, my grandmother took me with her to a 10-day "Sing Week" given by the Trapp Family in Stowe, Vermont. There I was struck by seeing a Catholic family, a Catholic priest and Mass. A few years later I was drawn to visit Catholic Churches and read some pamphlets including one on our Lady of Fatima. Of course, Our Lady had to have a hand in this! I finally read a copy of Thomas Merton's *Seven Storey Mountain* that I asked someone to lend me because I saw the picture of a monk on the cover. I read of Merton's conversion and entrance into the Catholic Church. It was a revelation to me that people could and did convert and become Catholics. I was 17 when, with my mother's written permission, I took instructions and was baptized.

I was blessed to attend a small Catholic college in Massachusetts and be surrounded by other Catholics. Then just after I graduated, a friend introduced me to a priest who became my regular confessor. It has been wonderful how many holy priests have helped me over the years. I mentioned religious life to this priest, and his reply was that I would "make a good laywoman." And he was right; I wasn't at all ready for religious life then. And I gave up that dream.

A career at Oxford University Press as secretary and then librarian began. One day while listening to a talk at the 1980 National Catholic Charismatic Conference at Notre Dame, I suddenly understood with great clarity that one day I would be living in community. I thought it meant one of the lay charismatic communities being formed. The next year I went back to the Notre Dame Conference, and there I had a profound experience of being called to celibacy. But I still didn't realize this meant religious life.

Some years later, while in my late 40s, I celebrated my birthday by having dinner with a close friend and afterward we spent hours talking in her apartment. At the end of the evening, she confided that she had thought of being a sister in the home missions when we were younger, and I shared my long-ago dream of being a Poor Clare. While walking home that night, I was surprised at the deep pain I felt at not having a vocation and prayed in that pain that I could serve God as a layperson.

It was less than a year after this realization that the idea of a vocation was still a strong desire, that God told me that I did "have a vocation." For nine months after that night I prayed very hard wondering and asking if I had heard correctly. At the end of that time, I was led to a Franciscan sister to be my spiritual adviser and she confirmed that God was indeed calling me to religious life. After this meeting with Sr. Loretta Theresa, F.H.M., I knew it was time to find a community to enter. A religious vocation doesn't exist in a vacuum, but in a particular place.

I visited Poor Clare monasteries as well as a number of other communities. Everywhere I went it was the same. I didn't feel called there and the vocation director would say that "Yes, I did have a vocation; just not to their community." One Benedictine vocation director even asked why I was there when I "prayed like a Franciscan."

One Scripture verse that I read and prayed over many times during this time of searching was the one in which Abraham obeyed God's call "without knowing where he was to go." Sarah received strength to conceive, despite being past the age, because she judged "He who had promised would keep faith." (Hebrews 11:8, 11)

Finally I went to a vocation discernment day led by Fr. Benedict Groeschel. During an hour of Eucharistic Adoration, I was filled with the light of knowing that my vocation was to the Poor Clares; and at the same moment I was filled with joy. For days afterward, that joy stayed with me especially when I thought the words "Poor Clares."

With renewed hope, I wrote several other Poor Clare monasteries on the East Coast. I was advised to write to Evansville, and this time I had the inspiration to ask my spiritual adviser to write them also. At last, after visiting so many places that I knew weren't right for me, at Evansville my spirit felt at home. During an interview with Sr. Anna, I asked if I could enter there. I returned home on June 29 and on August 15 the longed-for letter arrived saying I could enter and try my vocation.

When I first arrived at the monastery I was so pleased with living in the country that in good weather I took a bowl of cereal and ate breakfast outdoors. I could hardly wait until spring to grow my first flowers.

What keeps me here is a sense that I belong here and belong in monastic life. When there are tough times I can remember all the places I visited that I knew weren't right for me. Sometimes while we are praying the Divine Office together, I am visited with a beautiful sense of rightness that praying the Office in common is part of my life. There are so many good and joyful times with my sisters, and I know it is God's grace that I feel at home in community after 31 years of happily living alone.

There is another verse I treasure. At the very beginning of my search for a community, I went to a Mass for all the Manhattan prayer groups. It was February, near Valentine's Day. During the Mass, we were each handed a paper heart, red on one side and a Scripture verse on the other. Mine said: "In my Father's house there are many dwelling places; otherwise, how could I have told you that I was going to prepare a place for you? I am indeed going to prepare a place for you and then I shall come back to take you with me, that where I am you also may be." (John 14: 2-3). As I was reading this verse during Mass, at the very same time, I clearly understood that yes, there are many religious communities and many of them would not be right for me or I for them. But there was at least one community that would be and that Jesus would not be speaking to me about religious life if this were not so. He was preparing a place for me. How often that encouraged me as I continued my long search.

Sister Catherine Kiske Janeway, O.S.C.
Evansville, Indiana

"Time and again we willingly bound ourselves to our Lady, most holy Poverty, that after my death, the Sisters, those present and those to come, would never turn away from her."   *TestCl 39*

Autumn Leaves

Having grown up in Cincinnati, Ohio, autumn has always been my favorite season of the year. The front yard of my childhood home was graced with large oak and maple trees. The reward of raking the multitude of leaves was the thrilling leap to the center of the pile, to be covered in gold, russet and multicolored glory.

Now I have returned to Cincinnati in the autumn years of my life. I have experienced the magnificent springs of Memphis, Tennessee, the mountain seasons of Huehuetenango, Guatemala and the summers of Louisville, Kentucky.

The call to religious life started for me as a child raised in a German Catholic section of Cincinnati. The back of my home faced a large wooded area. I had "my apple tree." There I pondered the mysteries of life. With the tree, and visits to Gethsemani, the Trappist Monastery near Louisville, Kentucky, my contemplative vocation took seed.

The Sisters of Mercy staffed the grade school I attended. So when I was a sophomore in high school, and felt a pull in my heart to "leave all," I chose the Sisters of Mercy. My brother said I would never persevere as a nun because I couldn't get up early in the morning. My mom's advice was to stay at least until Christmas, and my father said: "You always have a home here." That was 42 years ago.

My years as a teaching sister were happy, full years for me. However, the inner voice of yearning for quiet prayer, silence and solitude wouldn't go away. In 1974 I transferred from the Sisters of Mercy to the Poor Clare Community in Memphis, Tennessee.

In 1979 Bishop Victor Hugo Martinez of Huehuetenango, Guatemala asked the community in Memphis to consider making a foundation in his department. In 1981 I was part of the group of five Poor Clares who settled in Huehuetenango, and built a monastery there. The experience with the poor and suffering people of Guatemala deepened my spiritual life in a way I could have never imagined. Here I was in the midst of a civil war. We were not able to move into the monastery because of the unrest in the country. The church people were being killed. We were told to have an escape route planned and a small bag packed. A military coup changed leadership in the country, and allowed us to move into the monastery and continue the life of St. Clare among the people of Huehuetenango.

While praying there on the eve of the New Year of 1987, I heard a voice saying: "I want you to bring the Poor Clares to Cincinnati." I was naturally taken aback and didn't do anything for a while. The prayer experience did not go away, so I shared it with my abbess.

After prayer and discernment, with the blessing of the leadership of the Poor Clare federations, and the communities in Huehuetenango and Memphis, I was given hospitality with the friars of the John the Baptist Province in Cincinnati. This was Advent 1989.

By June 1990 two other Poor Clares had answered a call to begin a foundation in Cincinnati and the seed of Clarian life was planted. The community now numbers eight, with the possibility of several more in the near future. The whole Franciscan family has nurtured this plan in so many and varied ways. In 1998, a beautiful new monastery was dedicated to serve the people of the Cincinnati diocese. The dream of bringing the Clares to Cincinnati is being fulfilled.

As for the future? These autumn years will continue to be as rich as the spring and summer ones have proven to be. I am sure I will be wrapped in joy, abundant and overflowing.

Sister Doris Gerke, O.S.C.
Cincinnati, Ohio

"And moved by compassion for us, he (Francis) bound himself...to always have the same loving care and special solicitude for us as for his own brothers."
TestCl 29

The Call

One day in my young life I was able to stand up and proclaim with the Bride of the **Song of Songs**: *I am black, but lovely* (Song of Songs 1:5); for though I was steeped in sin and black with it, I saw within the beauty of my baptism: the Father, the Son and the Holy Spirit.

For the dust of this world cannot forever hide the *treasure* (Matthew 13:52) of God and when I turned to prayer—not the prayer of outward observance but the prayer of the heart—I found the kingdom of God. I came upon the fine *pearl of great value* (Matthew 13:45-46).

Looking back at the beginnings of my conversion is rather like seeing the start of the journey from a great distance, or seeing the difficult climb from the heights of the mountain. Grace preceded and precipitated the moment I saw the Kingdom of God and was present thereafter. It was as though Jesus had said to his Father regarding my soul: *Give me time to dig around it and manure it: it may bear fruit....*(Luke 13:8-9).

From the perspective of years, then, I see that before my conversion I suffered. Yes, I suffered, but it was less from my own emptiness than from the longing of God within me. For vocation is a calling, an urgent cry from the God of desire, the Bridegroom: *Come then, my love, my lovely one, come...let me hear your voice; for your voice is sweet and your face is beautiful* (Song of Songs 2:13-14). And again: *I have come to bring fire to the earth and how I wish it were blazing already!* (Luke 12:49-50).

I felt within my bones and experienced that to ignore the desire of God is to become a slave of human desires, a slave of sorrow. I could say with Jeremiah: *"I will not speak in his name any more. Then there seemed to be a fire burning in my heart, imprisoned in my bones."* (Jeremiah 20:9).

This pain, sadness and depression was at its depths the longing of our God. Jesus proclaimed to me: *"You ravish my heart, my sister, my promised bride* (Song of Songs 4:9). He, the Bread of my soul, spoke to me as He had spoken at the Last Supper: *I have longed to eat this Passover with you before I suffer...."* (Luke 22:15).

When I discovered this longing, this love and fire of God within, I began to love and keep His holy law; and in turn, to know Him more and more: *"Anybody who receives my commandments and keeps them will be the one who loves me, and anybody who loves me will be loved by my Father and I shall love him and show myself to him."* (John 14:21).

The sight of Jesus within impelled me to exclaim with John and Andrew: *"Lord, where do you dwell?"* And Jesus gently replied: *"Come and see"* (John 1:35). So it was to the tabernacle that I came and before the Blessed Sacrament that my vocation was revealed to me.

Daily now, in my chosen vocation as a contemplative nun, I come before Him *whom my heart loves* (Song of Songs 1:7). In living this life of prayer and sacrifice for the Church and the world, I affirm that no suffering has been greater than the unrequited longing of God within and no joy greater than the daily finding of *Him whom my heart loves* (Song of Songs 3:4).

Sister Mary Kathleen McGarry, O.S.C.
Alexandria, Ontario, Canada

"Gaze upon that mirror (Jesus) each day, O Queen and Spouse of Jesus Christ and continually study your face within that you may adorn yourself within and without with beautiful robes covered, as is becoming the daughter and most chaste bride of the Most High King, with the flowers and garments of all the virtues."   *4LAg 15-17*

Freedom in Enclosure

When I was ten years old my father built the Poor Clare Monastery of Jeju Island. Little did I know then that 15 years later I would enter that monastery.

People ask me how I received my vocation. I always tell them that I received my calling while working in the courthouse offices. There I would see many prisoners in handcuffs unable to move to go about freely. They had lost all their outward freedom. They were unable to go and come as they wished. This made me think about inner freedom. I wanted to discover what true freedom meant.

In 1989 I entered the Monastery here. Strangely in this enclosed life I found I was freer than before. Here in prayer my heart could meet and enfold all my beloved family, friends and the whole world in a way I could never have done before.

For twelve years I enjoyed this freedom but I kept anguishing about why I was called here. What was my purpose for living here? In October 2002 I finally found my answer. I was sleeping in my room when I heard a voice inside me say: "You have received so much of God's mercy; now you must show others God's mercy." I jumped up, very surprised. I had to quickly write this message down so I would not forget it. I was so happy and relieved I cried and cried. I realized God was so immense. I was only now beginning to know just a little of God. I know one thing for sure. I breathe God's love and mercy. I walk in God's love and mercy, and I can embrace each Sister in this love and mercy. I want to love God more and more.

I am now the director of Postulants. As I meet these young women, I see in them a great fervor. This is good and I can understand them; and yet I want to convey to them this immense and overflowing mercy and love God gives to us despite the fact that we are unworthy of this grace. It doesn't depend on our great burning love or our fervor. God sends the rain and sunshine on the good and the bad alike. I want to teach the ones entrusted to me about this greatness of God, and my greatest fear is that I will not be able to do so. And yet this fear I also entrust to Our Lord and our Blessed Mother. With this comes peace. In their own time I trust God will teach each one as I have been taught.

Sister Paulina Kim, O.S.C.

Jeju Island, Korea

"When you have loved Him, you are chaste."   *1LAg 8A*

Zapped by God

Though I was not baptized as a baby, I never thought of myself as a convert. My father was not Catholic, and my parents had not been married in the Catholic Church. My older sister, my twin brother and I had not been baptized as babies and did not receive the sacraments, though we always went to Mass, ate fish on Fridays and observed similar practices with our mother and her Irish mother, who lived with us. I knew it was just a matter of time before I would become a full-fledged member of the Church.

The perfect opportunity came when a new young priest came to our parish with the intention of starting a CYO or Catholic Youth Organization. My brother, one of my girlfriends and I attended the first meeting of the young people in our parish and then asked this priest for private instructions in the Faith; our classes would be in the evenings as often as homework would permit. I found it fascinating to be learning so much about God's love and God's ways, and I looked forward to when I would become baptized. My classes began in February of my junior year of high school and my baptism took place on the Solemnity of Our Lady's Assumption, August 15th.

It was the following year on May 16th that Bishop Coleman F. Carroll of Miami confirmed me in Ft. Lauderdale, Florida. I had no idea how extraordinary that day would be, but my life was changed forever! As soon as the bishop placed the oil on my forehead, it seemed as though God said: "You're mine now." Since God was always so special in my life, how else was I to understand this, other than God wishes for me to become a nun? I took this very seriously and immediately stopped wearing makeup, buying clothes and dating. Of course, my family thought that was excessive, but it made logical sense to me if my life was going in a different direction now. I have learned that God can work softly and slowly in one's heart or God can "knock us off our horse" as was done to St. Paul. God had to work quickly though gently with me, and I still had lots of homework to do. It turned out that for four years I was like a fish out of water, not knowing where to go.

Already scheduled for junior college in Broward County, I attended for more than a year, as I discerned where God was calling me. Not having had nuns in school as my teachers, I was really at a loss for where to go. I made retreats at the Cenacle House in Lantana; however, the Cenacle Sisters required two years of college before entrance. Another community, Our Lady of Victory Missionary Sisters, was attractive to me after I took a course with them in preparation to teach Confraternity of Christian Doctrine in my parish. I eventually attended a weekend with young women interested in joining that community and I applied to enter. They asked me to wait another year, when they learned that I had only been baptized two years, though I had told them

I was not truly a "convert" or new to the Faith.

God gave me the grace to believe that His plans and His timing were trustworthy and after I began working full-time, I learned of an opportunity to make a pilgrimage to Our Lady's shrines in Fatima and Lourdes. Borrowing money from family and a friend, I made my way with a group of people from the Blue Army of Our Lady of Fatima. While we were in Lourdes we had been hearing over and over of Our Lady's request for prayer and penance for the conversion of sinners. I came to believe that God was asking me to give up everything and to enter a hidden life of prayer and penance for my salvation and the salvation of others. I had no doubt in my mind! I remember thinking that now I would not be tempted to "make a name for myself" and all of the glory would go to God.

But where would I go into the cloister? I visited the Carmelite community in Roxbury, Massachusetts but then learned of the Poor Clare Monastery in Delray Beach, Florida. After hearing in my parish of their open house before their new monastery would be dedicated, my sister and my mother joined me in "exploring" this monastery that was practically in my own back yard. We had a tour of the monastery and especially liked seeing where the altar breads were made. Though I had loads of questions, it seemed as though my sister was the one being eyed by the Poor Clare who was showing us around. Before I knew it,

I was coming to visit in the parlor, first with the Abbess and then with the young sisters from the Novitiate. That really sealed it when I saw how they teased with one another and seemed so "normal." I thought I might just fit in…despite the fact that the building was so new and so big and they even had their own icemaker! I cringe when I think of some of the hang-ups I had (still have?) God has been so very generous to me and so patient as I came to know and accept God's mercy and wisdom in my life.

When I became a Franciscan I found my true self and true calling. I cannot imagine where I would be if I had not answered God's generous and magnificent invitation to leave all — and thereby receive All. God is so good! What a joy it is to live with one's eyes "fixed on Jesus" with Saints Clare and Francis as mirrors and models!

Sister Frances Vass, O.S.C.
Delray Beach, Florida.

"Gaze upon Him; consider Him; contemplate Him, as you desire to imitate Him." 2LAg 20b

I'm His...Hook...Line...And Sinker!

I come from a Catholic family, the second of five children. My oldest sister became a Notre Dame Sister, and all I ever wanted was to be married and have at least a dozen children. Religious life passed through my mind for a brief moment when, at 16, I was only going to go so I could see my sister. I missed her terribly. Little did I know then that Our Lord had His plans for my life.

After an unsuccessful marriage and years of working through that pain, my son and I moved to Coral Springs, Florida, in July 1985, and we started a new life there. I was doing okay until my son went on drugs and I was almost out of my mind with fear. I didn't have even a little idea of how to help him or where to turn. I literally crawled into San Isidro Catholic Charismatic Church in Pompano Beach, and there I found Jesus. I had never had an intimate relationship with Our Lord. Although I went to Mass each Sunday, I didn't really **know** God.

The men and women of my parish in Florida were Jesus to me. They showed me His love, kindness, gentleness and understanding at a moment in my life when I wasn't sure I could go on...so much pain, Lord. Too much pain, Lord. We were blessed with three priests who fed us daily with how much God loves us, and I was like a sponge soaking in every word. I grew ever closer to our Lord, even going to Mass each morning. Sometimes on my lunch hour, I'd drop by church for a visit. I couldn't get enough of our Lord Jesus. I was His...hook, line and sinker.

In November 1990 I made a Cursillo weekend and I had no idea what to expect. It was a wonder-filled experience. The following weekend I went to my spiritual director, Fr. Antonio, and told him I had to write a letter and I needed an address. He told me to come by the Rectory in the morning; he would help me. After our special time together, he suggested I go over to the Parish Hall as a Secular Franciscan friend was there waiting to see Father as soon as I left. I had heard that she was going to become a nun and move to Texas, and I told her how happy I was for her. She was so excited as she shared how she had been in touch with the Sisters for two years. However, she was not well and you had to be in good health to join the Poor Clares. I asked her if I called her on Sunday if she would give me the address. She said: "Are you going to join too? I responded emphatically, "**No**...but I have to write a letter."

After we parted, I went into church and knelt before Our Lord in the tabernacle. I hugged Him close to me as I gave Him thanks for not calling me to be a nun. "I'll do whatever you ask of me, Lord. I'm so glad you didn't call me to be a nun. Where do you want me to go Lord; tell me and I'll do it." To my total astonishment, I heard **His** voice saying, in the quiet of my heart: "That's where I want you to go. I want you to go to Texas and be with the Poor." My next-to-instant response was, "Yes, Lord, I'll go. I'll do as you ask." And no sooner had I gotten the words out, then I felt a surge of inner joy, a burst like nothing I had ever experienced, radiating through my entire body. I felt like I could have lit up the city! And it was then for sure that I knew this was from Our Lord.

How blessed I felt and so completely overwhelmed that Our Lord would call me to such an incredible vocation. When friends stopped by during the Peace Sign at Mass and asked why I was crying, I said: "He's calling me to leave here. He's calling me away." And they assured me that that couldn't be...after all, this was my second home. It's great to be loved so much!

I called my friend on Sunday for the address of the Poor Clare Monastery in Victoria, Texas. On Monday I wrote a letter to Sr. Gabriel telling her of what had happened. Her response was precious. At some point she asked me how long I had had a vocation, and I responded that I did not have a vocation. I just needed to talk with her. She included a brochure about the community and I gave a copy of it to my precious Father Antonio. I told him I wasn't sure what it was all about but I felt that was where I was supposed to go. Padre confirmed that the next morning after Mass: He said: "That's where you're supposed to be."

I wrote some more to Sr. Gabriel and asked if I could come for a visit. We set it up for May 1991, a visit of nine days. From the minute I met the Sisters, I felt like I had come home. After no time at all, it seemed like we had been friends for years. I loved everything about them and their life of prayer and community and sharing with the larger community. They gave me an application and I began the process to see if I could be a member of their Order. I returned home with a tentative return date of September 1. On a Saturday night around 8:30 p.m., the end of June 1991, the phone rang, and it was Sr. Antoinette telling me I had been accepted. The Sisters all got on the phone and congratulated me. It was an alleluia moment. Then I hopped in my car and drove over to church just as Fr. Antonio finished the evening Mass. He was thrilled for me. At his suggestion I returned jubilantly to one of my favorite places at the tabernacle with Our Lord in the Blessed Sacrament to thank Him. I knew in my heart that only His grace could make all this happen.

Our Lord gave me the next two months to spend special unforgettable time with my spiritual family and my son...to say our good-byes; to part with all my possessions, taking the money and giving it to the poor...and the more I gave, the richer I felt.

Friday, September 6th I flew on to Victoria. The sisters greeted me at the plane. I was home, and I felt so good to be here. I went on to be admitted as a postulant on September 17; one year later I became a novice and received the name Sister Katherine of the Most Precious Blood of Jesus. I made first vows in 1994, and my solemn profession was on August 15, 1998. That was one of the most incredible days in my life. Having my son walk me down the aisle was a joyous moment for me. As I vowed to my Lord that I would live my life in poverty, chastity, obedience and enclosure, I became overwhelmed with His joy. Truly an alleluia moment!

I'm honored to have been called by Our Lord to serve Him as a Poor Clare Sister. Texas is a wonderful place to live. I love Victoria. The people here are so respectful, loving, friendly and warm.

During my years of formation, there were many physical obstacles in my life. With the grace of God and an incredible spirit of perseverence, I came to see them all not as obstacles but as opportunities. In looking back, I know now that Our Lord was with me and carrying me on all those very painful days. May God be praised! During my 13 years here, Our Lord has sent many wonderful people into my life to help me along my journey: my spiritual family and my new family in Victoria: Priests, Poor Clares, Spiritual Directors, counselors and many friends. I am truly blessed.

During that time there were also some unbelievably painful times when sorrow from my childhood came to light and had to be dealt with. Again, Our Lord sent wonderful counselors and friends to help me along the way.

Today, my life is blessed. I can finally say with all my heart: "Thank you, God, for the pain and suffering." God's grace was there for me on a daily basis. Working through the pain has made me a very strong woman. I am now able to help hurting men and women God continues to send to me who are struggling with the same issues I had. My pain was not in vain. It was truly for the glory of God. Thank you, dear Lord and St. Clare, for honoring me and judging me worthy of being chosen to be one of your Poor Clare Sisters. Franciscan joy abounds in my heart!

Sister Katherine, O.S.C.
Victoria, Texas

"...loving one another with the charity of Christ, may the love you have in your hearts be shown outwardly in your deeds so that...the sisters may always grow in love of God." TestCl 59, 60

With God, Nothing is Impossible

"What a great and praiseworthy exchange: to leave the things of time for those of eternity, to choose the things of heaven for the goods of the earth, to receive the hundred-fold in place of one, and to possess a blessed and eternal life!" (St. Clare)

I had a headache as I looked into the mirror. I was in my second year of university and I had been up all night, drinking with my friends. The sun was just starting to come up, but the curtains covering the windows in my little room in the Vancouver School of Theology dorm, where I was boarding on the University of British Columbia campus, were still drawn and the light was soft.

After looking into the mirror, I sat down on the floor and sobbed. I didn't like what I was becoming. I loved my friends; they were good people, and we were all good students. I was tired of the drinking and the dirty jokes. What upset me the most was that in actual fact I wasn't tired of it; I loved it.

There weren't any limits anymore. I could go as far as I wanted to, but for what? Everything was so empty. The Lord had called to me in my heart about approaching the faith once before this day, but I had said no, and had run for all I could. Not this time, however, as that mirror was a turning point for me, one that in time led me into the loving contemplation of the true mirror in my life.

My "story" actually began as my life began, with the beads of past years threaded together. A battle with cancer in my early childhood was followed by years of good health and grace with my beautiful family, parents and a brother. We lived on a little sheep farm in Mt. Lehman, B.C., and in later years on the waterfront of Vancouver Island, being nurtured and steeped in a deep love for nature, from the mountains to the sea, and fostered in school and at home with the gifts of art and music.

As an infant my uncle, an Oblate of Mary Immaculate, baptized me a Catholic although I grew up knowing nothing of my faith. I attended Mass infrequently as a child and very seldom in my teenage years. I never knew it was Christ I was receiving, and I never received the Sacrament of Reconciliation or ever knew I should — and yet He was always there.

I always tell people now, and truthfully, that I loved Him long before I ever knew Him. My heart was always waiting and longing...for something.

I got up off the floor of my room that morning at UBC and never turned back. It wasn't long before I discovered St. Mark's Basilian chapel on campus and began receiving daily Communion. It was sitting there in that little chapel that I first found all I had ever hoped and waited for.

Even before I knew He was truly present in His Body and His Most Precious Blood, I knew in my heart that He was there. It was as if the truths of the Catholic faith had always been a part of me. I made many new friends and how patiently and lovingly they carried me in those first months of conversion.

It was while driving back to UBC one day after a visit to Westminster Abbey in Mission that a friend turned to me and said that I really ought to go and see the Poor Clares. "The poor what?" I asked. I wasn't thinking of a religious vocation; I just needed some help carrying an extra heavy cross.

I met the Poor Clares in November 1994. That same month, still at UBC, I woke up with the very clear realization that God wanted me to be a nun. Once again, of course, I gave the perfect answer, "No, absolutely not." As you may have guessed, however, that's not where the story ended. I went on a three-day vocation retreat (the first of many) at the Poor Clares the following January. I was attracted at once by the richness of their life of prayer, their simplicity, their joyful Franciscan spirit and most especially to the Poor Clare charism of Gospel poverty, which seemed to fulfill all the deepest longings of my heart. At the end of that first retreat, I went up to the abbess and said that I wanted to enter.

I was confirmed at Holy Rosary Cathedral in June 1995, graduated from UBC in 1996 with a BA in art history and in the fall of the same year spent a few months at the Madonna House lay apostolate in Combermere, Ontario. At the age of 22, I entered the monastery here in Mission on January 3, 1997, the feast of the holy Name of Jesus and made my solemn profession six years later on January 3, 2003.

I desire nothing more than to spend my life as a witness to the one Truth, and as a living prayer and oblation for the love of the Poor Crucified, our Holy Mother Church, and for the salvation of every soul. I offer the small gift of my youth as a sign to give courage and hope to any young person, so challenged by the darkness of our times, to listen and hear within their hearts the firm and gentle calling of Christ, "Come, follow Me...Be not afraid."

Sister Laura Marie Swoboda, O.S.C.
Mission, B.C., Canada

"May you cling to His most sweet Mother who gave birth to a Son whom the heavens could not contain."   *3LAg 18*

PART 1: *"I Heard the Voice of Jesus Say..."*

The Story Of My Conversion

First of all, I am a convert. Also, I was an Army nurse in WWII. I was baptized at a 9 a.m. Mass in the Chapel of the 191st General Army Hospital located a little south of Paris, France on Christmas Eve 1944.

At the time I did not recognize the fact that I received a Religious Vocation with the gift of Faith. It took 30 years to fulfill that vocation.

Both my parents were ill, and being an only child I was not free to enter religious life until they died. They died nine weeks apart.

The day my mother died, December 18, 1973, I started to pray to know God's will for me. I told Him I wanted to be consecrated to Him in some way. I said if He would make it crystal clear to me what He wanted, with the help of His grace, I would do it.

The answer came on Epiphany: "Go to the Poor Clares." When I got home from Mass, I phoned Sister Emmanuel to ask if I might see her that afternoon if possible. We met that afternoon and Sister Emmanuel said they would have a community meeting in two weeks; I would hear from her at that time. The letter of acceptance came in 10 days.

I was working in a nursing home at the time. Immediately I went to the phone and gave a month's notice. Then I phoned a friend in real estate and put my small house on the market. As I was waiting for the phone to be answered, I remember thinking, I am cutting completely every bit of financial support. Yet I remember looking up and saying: "God, what You start You can finish."

You must understand I had no other income except my job. My parent's illnesses had used up every bit of savings we had. I was 52 and it was a risky business to be starting something that you did not know how it would turn out. Yet God made it crystal clear, so now I lived up to my promise to depend on His grace to fulfill the vocation.

March 15, 2003 was the 29th year from entry into the Poor Clares. In 2002, at the age of 80, I celebrated my 25th Jubilee (counting from first vows in 1977). God will always live up to His promises. This vocation is a real testament and witness to God's love, grace and mercy. There are not the words to say how grateful I am now and for all past years of being a Poor Clare.

Sister Margaret Fackler, O.S.C.
Delray Beach, Florida

"When you have touched Him, you become more pure."   *1LAg 8b*

It Happened In a Castle

My story begins in a castle. Yes, the Benedictine Monastery in Ferdinand, Indiana was called The Castle on the Hill. It dominated the hill, and overlooked the town of Ferdinand. The Benedictine Sisters had an academy for girls which I attended. It was my sophomore year.

The question had come up, as it does for any Catholic girl, "Are you going to be a nun?" My answer was a definite "No!" For one thing, I was an only child. My mother had died young, and I planned on taking care of my dad in his old age. The Sisters had insisted on this in grade school, that we had a duty to our parents to look after them when they were old. I took it very seriously. I would get married, raise a family, and then take my dad in when he got old.

Man proposes; God disposes. It was a rainy, cold, blustery Sunday, sometime between Christmas and Easter vacation. Because of the weather, several from our sophomore class had gathered in the small study hall, sitting around talking. It was a hangout for our class. As we got to talking, several of us remarked how great it was that five of our class were going to enter the convent. None of us saying this intended entering, though. As Lucille walked in the room, a couple of us looked up and said, "Here comes Sister Lucille." It was no secret that she intended entering the convent at Ferdinand. Lucille asked what this was all about. I spoke up and told her what we had been talking about, and that five of our class were entering the convent. I proceeded to name them. She looked at me and said, "You missed one." I asked, "Who?" And she replied, "You." To make it all the more ridiculous, I replied, "Oh, sure! A Poor Clare yet!" In other words, let's make this as ridiculous as possible. As far as I was concerned, that was the end of that.

That night, in study hall, I was going over the events of the day as usual. When I recalled that conversation, Lucille's remark and my answer, a voice said, as clear as if spoken out loud, "Why not?" My reply was, "What do you mean, why not?" And with that, I started to give all the reasons "why not" to the Lord. First of all, I had to take care of my dad. Then, that kind of life wasn't for me. After all, I was a tomboy, loved to ride horses, go swimming, and hiking, the outdoors in general.

Being from Evansville, Indiana, I was aware of the Poor Clares there, and of the high wall around the monastery. I also knew of them because the Extern Sisters would come to my dad's grocery store once a month, begging for any food that he would give them. Probably my dad had told me about them, also.

As a Poor Clare, I would have to spend my life within one square city block, never ride a horse again, or go swimming, or target practice, or enjoy roaming over our farm, or pick blackberries, or enjoy my dad's company, playing pool with him, painting the house, varnishing the pool room floor, and all those kinds of things. No, the cloistered life was definitely out. Not for me. No way.

But the voice, once heard, could not be denied.

And now, having celebrated my golden jubilee as a Poor Clare, I have to admit the Lord knew what He was doing.

Sister Olivia Wassmer, O.S.C.
New Orleans, Louisiana

"Be filled with a remarkable happiness and a spiritual joy."   *1LAg 21b*

The Rich Life!

Mary, whenever I try to get to know you better, you point out something away from yourself. You redirect my thoughts to something your Son is doing, and how He is always being for me. Your statement to the servant at Cana to: "Do whatever He tells you" (John 2:6) is one of my favorites it seems. Sometimes He doesn't tell me anything; He is singularly there for me. Mary, you keep yourself so very much in the background that His glory shines so, I can hardly see you. That's your good example for me, isn't it?

I see our vocation as spanning a lifetime of ever changing and developing a personal relationship with God. God is Trinity. At various times He has been very much the Father. For instance, at ten years old, I quizzed Him relentlessly for an answer to all my "whys" after mother died. He answered me as a loving Father, indicating I must just trust Him. Other times when I felt very alone and poured out my self-pity to Him, it was Jesus who was listening and encouraging me while riding a bike alongside me. As Holy Spirit, He has responded and directed me through events or other people, or in my heart.

The litany of events that led me to serve Him as a Contemplative Poor Clare would take more words than time or space would allow here. I'm trying to describe something that words cannot adequately express. Love makes one want to give the other everything they could possibly want and more without being able to have enough to give.

At about 15 years old, I was sitting on the front steps telling our Lord of how unfair life was. My first love, the boy next door, had died of cancer. Telling the Lord that it seemed like everyone I got really close to, He took away to heaven and how was it He kept saying "Love one another...?" I had already lost an aunt after Mother and another classmate. He said: "I want all of you for Myself." After trying to figure that out as a young Methodist, I finally just let it go knowing that He wants to save everyone. Meanwhile there was this continuing inner pull to know Jesus better, to somehow get closer to Him. I thought that had been realized when graduation from nursing school happened and Confirmation into the Catholic Church happened the same year.

Some three years later, I found myself in South America as a missionary nurse for the Catholic Church as a layperson. I worked almost daily as a volunteer with a Mercy sister in the parish church activities. We became close friends and still are. When I told her I was praying about the contemplative life she told me she wasn't surprised at all! The mission volunteer contract was nearing the end and I was pleading to the Lord to show me whether to continue in the missions or return to the States.

As my stepmother was dying of cancer, there came the now familiar inner pull in my heart. Yes, this mission was going to end after 20 years with this well-loved person who had been so very good to me. I could feel a tug at my heart to learn about contemplative prayer. It felt like a gift all wrapped and waiting under the Christmas tree. I didn't want to unwrap it until after "mother" was gone so as not to be distracted in my care of her.

One day during Mass, our Pastor spoke strongly about becoming a priest or nun. Everything he said seemed directed at me. I thought, "How can I be a nun? I'm too old. Besides don't they have to enter at 20 or 22 in total innocence of the sins and bad language out here in the world? I've heard it all working in the ghetto as a visiting nurse."

A need became clear to get to know St. Clare better after learning about St. Francis. As I read about St. Clare and visited San Damiano in Assisi, I wanted to visit some Poor Clares of today and see what they were like and how they have changed over time. Also, a desire was beginning to grow in my heart to see if it would be possible for me to even think about becoming a Poor Clare. I laughed to even think of it, it seemed so absurd. Nonetheless, I pursued it. What if they actually confirmed my thinking?

My Spiritual Director advised me to visit other contemplative Orders. I dutifully visited the Good Shepherds and the Carmelites, but my Franciscan spirituality was too good a "fit" to want to give it up.

When my stepmother died, I thought I should wait about two years before making any big changes in my life. Actually this provided the time I needed to pray, talk with my spiritual director and generally develop some idea of where I was going.

When I first visited the Evansville Monastery, I told our Lord that I didn't think I deserved to be there. It was all too beautiful and simple, and total gift.

When I was received as a postulant, I could hardly contain myself in the freedom I experienced. I hadn't felt this free since I was six or seven years old before mother died. Of course, responsibilities would come, but it's all for You, Lord. It still seems so amazing. Now I understand some of what the Lord meant when He told me He wanted all of me for Himself, and I had asked how that would be since He was invisible and all Spirit and I wasn't. I'm trying to learn Lord. I remain committed to You and my sisters here, even if sometimes it doesn't look that way.

This is my fourteenth year of living in this Poor Clare Monastery, and my heart is ever grateful. Yes, Mary, your message is so simple yet so vast: "Do whatever He tells you." (John 2:6). The thing is to know if it's really Him or my own heart speaking to me!

Imagine being allowed to live this life. There is so much to learn, Lord! Help me become ever closer to You and be totally for You when You send the final call to see You face to face. For now I recall Your words that sang in my heart following first Profession: "...my cup overflows. Only goodness and kindness follow me all the days of my life. And I shall dwell in the house of the Lord for years to come," (Ps. 23:5-6), and I add, all the days of my life. Amen, Alleluia.

Sister Jane Marie DeLand, O.S.C.
Evansville, Indiana

"When you have accepted Him, you are a virgin."   *1LAg 8c*

My Soul

Praise the Lord, O my Soul! And all that is within me,
Praise His Holy Name!

My Soul, — given to me with the touch of Your creation

My Soul, — small and unformed

My Soul, — born and nurtured, breathed into with Your
Breath of Life

My Soul, — blessed with the Kiss of Your Holy Spirit

My Soul, — fed and formed in the Love of your Son

My Soul, — small and battered about in the lessons of
life in the world

My Soul, — smudged and tattered by following poor choices

My Soul, — supported and carried by Jesus through
His Mother

My Soul, — unclean, washed, unclean, washed

My Soul, — so little of it, if any that is pure to be offered to
the Father

PART 1: *"I Heard the Voice of Jesus Say..."*

My Soul, — led and ever so gently caressed by my Mother Mary

My Soul, — if I give myself to my Father where does the "I" go

My Soul, — overwhelmed in the experience of Jesus' Love

My Soul, — surrender yourself

Soul? — Yes!

Sister Jane Marie DeLand, O.S.C. 9-93

We are greatly bound to bless and praise God and be all the more strengthened to do good in the Lord."   *TestCl 22*

The Evangelical Life of Saint Clare

'Come Follow Me'

For many women in the early 13th century the voice of Jesus said, "Come follow me." At the time of Clare of Assisi there was a vigorous women's movement that was independent of the male religious orders in the Church. In the 12th century women entered or were placed in Benedictine, Cistercian, or Norbertine monasteries and were under the jurisdiction of male superiors. At the beginning of the13[th] century women were forming independent groups in what was referred to as the women's poverty movement in central and northern Italy. In the Low Lands these groups were called beguines. It is intriguing to wonder why there was such a movement at this particular moment in history.

The 13th century saw the beginning of a shift from a gift economy to a profit economy, from paying for goods and services by means of barter to that of a cash system. It was the beginning of capitalism. Did these women intuit the potential for the degeneration of a society where monetary gain was placed before the mutuality of human relationships? Did they want to speak with their lives the relative value of wealth and what it promised to provide? In the shift moments of history the underclass sees potential for change. Perhaps these women saw the possibility of a new form of Christian commitment in response to the call of Jesus in the gospel. In this volatile social climate Clare met with Francis of Assisi to discuss the future of their mutual gospel project.

Clare began her form of life with her sister, Agnes, and other young women of the area, in partnership with Francis and his early friars but never under the jurisdiction of the Franciscans. Clare wrote in the Rule of 1253 that from the beginning of their life at San Damiano they had at least four friars with them, a priest, a cleric and two lay brothers. It is interesting to note that the clericalization of the Franciscans began in 1239 and by 1260, as laid down in The Constitutions of Narbonne, the lay brothers were all but excluded from admittance in the Franciscan Order. By 1263 this provision in the Rule of Clare for participation of lay brothers in the life of the sisters no longer mattered. The Rule of Pope Urban IV was promulgated and began to quickly supersede the Rule of Clare.

Just as the Franciscans became an order of priests the "poor sisters that the Blessed Father Francis established" became, in the Rule of Urban, the "Order of St. Clare." In his Rule the Pope decreed, "It is lawful for you to receive and to have in common possessions and revenues and to freely retain them." The Abbess was directed to hire a lay procurator to properly administer the properties and revenues belonging to the monastery. The daring charism of the founding moment of Clarian life had been domesticated. It was now unrecognizable from generic monastic life for women.

This, of course, was not the end of the story but the beginning of renewal movements down through the centuries to our own times exemplified by these vocation stories....

I'm His...From Forever

Sharings from the earliest moments of life.

My Vocational Story

One might say that my story has a touch of the extraordinary as I took God very seriously from ages five or six. I was taken regularly to Church and to Mass from the time I was three or four. At seven my special attraction was the saints and, of course, Saint Clare came to my attention! When I was ten, I had learned that the women who followed the Rule of Clare did not perform the tasks of other religious women serving in the active apostolate, but that their whole day was spent living in simplicity, prayer, adoration and penance. I was so impressed that I wrote to the Monastery at the age of ten! The desire to serve other people was also present.

At thirteen, I joined the Aspiranture of the School Sisters of Notre Dame who taught me. I became very homesick and returned home to attend the high school taught by the same sisters. My high school days were a time of discernment in regard to the call to which I believed God was inviting me. The desire to belong totally and unconditionally to the Lord took hold of me! I was advised to take Latin in school so that I may be able to read the Divine Office. I worked a year after high school, making frequent trips to the nearest Monastery of Poor Clares on Hollywood Avenue. I was convinced this was where God wanted me; yet, to be certain, I investigated other contemplative communities such as the Visitation and Carmelite monasteries.

After prayer, I decided that the Poor Clare way of life was the most joyful penitential lifestyle for me. On September 8, 1963, I entered the monastery in the Bronx, New York. Like Saint Therese, I said: "Now I am here forever and ever!" It seemed to me that I entered a way of life that would never change! The midnight office, long vocal prayers, the constant penance of community life, silence and withdrawal from the world (meaning for me, family and friends) filled my heart with such joy! At the very beginning of my religious life, the thought that sustained my union with God was the mystery of the Blessed Trinity living within us. It is still a conviction that gives meaning to my life! The other factor in my spiritual life was and is the Blessed Virgin. From childhood I was told I was named just for Mary as I was born in May and on a Saturday.

Then came Vatican II. Actually the Council had begun several years before, but now it became evident that we, as contemplatives were in for a few changes. I was just learning about Saint Clare's charism; now it was being re-thought and re-taught as part of the Franciscan charism. For me it was a confusing as well as an exciting time. I had to relearn what "separation from the world" really meant for today's world. What a surprise to realize that I was still in the world, even though I lived apart from its mainstream. Francis, who was part of Clare's charism, had a great love of the world and God's creation and it "was very good" because for Francis, God was "all good, the only good, the highest good!" (Rule 1221) By the time of my Solemn

Profession in 1970, the community had seen many changes, and I had too. We modified our habits, shortened our long vocal prayers and went about our tasks at a more contemplative pace. At the same time, classes in philosophy, theology, psychology, and scripture were introduced. With these changes came extra time for prayer and study. God gave me the grace to use this period of my life to come to a deeper understanding of myself but not without struggle. In my life at this time, human and Divine Love were seemingly at odds. They were at least within myself!

I arose from this test with a deep sense of the Lord's love and commitment to me as well as an appreciation of my ability to love as a woman and a Spouse of Christ. Shortly after this, I was given the opportunity to attend Nursing School to use for our community needs. This year of study gave me many experiences to draw on for my future life as a Clare. How wonderful to return to community and the choral recitation of the Liturgy of the Hours! With mind sharpened, love of study and reading seemed to come to fruition in me. For many years my main work would be in the infirmary. I treasured those years and identified very closely with Mother Clare, her illnesses coupled with her compassion and love for the sick and dying! Courses in spiritual direction and counseling aided me not only to help myself, but also others. My work with the Secular Franciscans who met at our monastery confirmed this for me.

In 1998, I became involved in formation work for the community. Prior to that I taught Liturgy and Franciscanism in the novitiate program. Working in formation has been such a grace and has taught me valuable lessons in the area. At times God's love seems overflowing in me; at other times God is at a distance.

Chardin speaks of the Lord's command to love all of the universe. He also cites those "special preferential loves that God sends into our lives" (*Hymn of the Universe*). This kind of loving enables us to go on when there seems to be more darkness than light across our path leading to God. He himself had a profound spiritual relationship with his blood sister Marguerite. She shared many of his scientific discoveries but it was the spiritual, which bound them most close.

It is in the love of special people in my life that the face of God has been revealed to me! I thank God for Chardin and the world-view he has left us. I often feel the words to Lady Poverty by the Brothers very appropriate when she asked to see their cloister: "The world is our cloister" (*Sacrum Commercium: #63*). These words of Mother Clare also become dearer to me each day: "Be lovers of your souls and of all your sisters" (*Blessing of Clare #14*) and "let the love you have in your hearts be shown in your deeds" (*Testament of Saint Clare #59*).

Our community from Hollywood Avenue is now in temporary quarters. It has been a difficult five years. However, it has taught me that we are always in a "temporary place until we are called home to heaven." We do not have here a lasting dwelling, no matter how beautiful the monastery. As Saint Augustine taught us: "Our true, my true resting place is in you, O Lord, and my heart is restless until it rests in You!" *(Confessions of Saint Augustine)*

Sister Mary Cecilia Keyser, O.S.C.
New Rochelle, New York

"Place your heart in the figure of the divine substance!"   *3LAg 13a*

Twenty-Four Sisters

It was the summer of sixth grade looking forward to the seventh, 1954, while I was in bed with mononucleosis or the "kissing disease" as I was teased, that I believe I first felt the stirrings of a religious calling. I was accustomed to going to our parish library and bringing home books. This time I brought home *My Beloved: The Story of a Carmelite Nun*. I trace my response nine years later, that of entering the Poor Clare monastery in the city of my birth, to that book selection.

What did Mother Catherine Thomas, the author of the book, say that had such a powerful impact on me? It was the philosophy about contemplative life that inspired me. She said that if a person was intimately connected to Christ Jesus they were helping Him save the world. Over and over she emphasized the power of prayer and the efficacy of a life dedicated to God for the good of others.

While I was growing up I had a recurring fantasy about going away to boarding school and receiving letters and care packages and being very special. I would muse about writing home and telling fantastic stories about the goings on at my new school. I am sure reading about a young woman going off to the convent wasn't very different in my imagination to that of going to a boarding school.

It is true that grace builds on nature, and God took my personality and strengths into consideration when He/She drew me to give myself as a Poor Clare Nun. I was the only daughter in my family and I longed for a baby sister, driving my parents crazy by begging for this. When I entered my mother commented that now God had given me 24 sisters!

I was idealistic and desirous of making a difference. I also carried something of a "wound" from childhood that felt I wasn't good enough and would make up what was lacking in me and in my world by suffering and offering up the good things of life for a better life. Now, nearly forty years later, I have discovered that it isn't my efforts or suffering that are effective, but God's unconditional love and regard that save the world and make us holy. I think God has been delighted though, and touched by my good will and intentions! I have no regrets but only gratitude for the numerous ways God has carved out a place within me that knows without a doubt that I am special and loved. I also believe that being members of Christ's own body we are affecting each other every second of every breath, and this is enough for me.

There are times I wonder why more women are not drawn to our beautiful way of life. What can be more meaningful than the spiritual journey and sharing this with sisters in community? Joy overflows in me when I am praying for others and praising God with gratitude and awe. My fantasies for boarding school and having a sister have been fulfilled and many, many more!

Sister Dianne Doughty, O.S.C.
Saginaw, Michigan

"Truly I can rejoice and no one can rob me of such joy." 3LAg 5

On Holy Ground

I was born July 7, 1945 in Kansas City, Missouri and baptized Margaret (though I was always called "Peggy") Jane Stretz on July 29. I can remember that, after receiving my First Communion preparations classes, I often asked my mother why she and Dad left me in original sin for three weeks instead of getting me off to church right away!

I attended St. Louis Grade School (K.C., Missouri) for primary education and remember vividly watching with the rest of my third grade class a slide presentation of St. Catherine Laboure and the Miraculous Medal. It was from that moment that I decided to be a Sister. Within the next year or two, after reading quite a number of the saint books from the school library, I discovered that there existed in the Church contemplative communities. They immediately caught my imagination since I felt fired up to do "hard" things for the Lord and arrive at sanctity as fast as I could! (I often think that all those great desires didn't combine with an ill humor often displayed toward my very wonderful sisters and brothers: Sharon, Sandy, Frank and John). By the time I reached high school I definitely decided to be a contemplative nun, having the Carmelites highest on the list.

My father, Frank, and my mother, Catherine Cushing, had to move us around frequently once my high school years began because of Dad's work with Chrysler. I ended up going to three different high schools. I would have graduated from a fourth but it was decided that I would stay put with a girlfriend and her family and finish my senior year in St. Louis, Missouri, while the family moved on to Memphis, Tennessee. One day I noticed in a book on Religious that there was a Monastery of Poor Clares in Memphis and decided to write to them during the summer after my graduation. Mother Paul (Novice Mistress) received my parents and me very graciously and I decided that I would enter the September of that year, knowing that my family would probably be moving on — after my entrance they did move on to Jacksonville, Florida.

I was sixteen when I graduated from high school due to the fact that I skipped seventh grade and went to eighth. The summer before I entered the Monastery my friend, Judy Jackson, came to visit me from K.C. My family and I lived quite close to Elvis Presley's house in Memphis so Judy and I decided to go up and watch him play touch football close to a field by his house. Although he was quite well known then, it was common to see him doing "ordinary" things like touch football. Judy and I were seated on the ground with other young people and during the "break" Elvis eyed Judy and me. He came up to us and asked me if

I would like his teeth guard. With great disgust I said, "Heavens, no!!!" (And to think I could have had millions for our missionary work here in Huehuetenango!)

When I entered on September 15, 1962, at 17 years of age, I thought I had landed on another planet. The customs were still — if not the middle ages — at least from the 1800's, and all my desires for the "hard" things went directly down the tubes. I was so homesick and missed my sisters and brothers more than I thought possible.

The years were very hard but all the Sisters so very good. I am very glad now that I had the opportunity to live the "before" and "after" years of the Second Vatican Council. What a difference the Council made! I think we're all still struggling with an evangelical response to a third millennium contemplative life. While we're searching, the Lord has already found us and it's "just" a matter of hearing what He says.

In 1981 Sister Mary Peter Rowland, Sister Mary Doris Gerke, Sister Mary Antonio, Sister Mary Claudia Phillips, Sister Mary Regina Likavec and I arrived in Huehuetenango, Guatemala, to begin a Monastery of Poor Clares by the invitation of Bishop Victor Hugo Martínez. Sister Peter and I decided to stay on with this mission while the Lord asked other labors of the four other founding Sisters. We now have three novices and one solemnly professed

Guatemalan. Putting down roots and trying to enter into the spirit of "inculturation" has been a tough and ongoing job. We feel its fruits! I pray the Lord will let me go to Him from this little spot of His planet, from this little spot of His holy ground.

Sister Mary Agnes Stretz, O.S.C.
Huehuetenango, Guatemala

"Offer faithfully what you have vowed to God and He shall reward you."
LEr 8

Loving Surrender To God's Will

When I think back on my path to embracing the vocation of a Poor Clare, I find a number of one-liners that spoke to my heart and eventually made an impression upon me.

From about the age of four I was faced with the issue of a religious vocation through my aunt, a religious sister and nurse. She questioned me as to whether I would like to be a nun when I grew up. Young as I was I did not appreciate her suggestive question and thought to myself, *no one is going to make up my mind for me* ! However the option remained with me and I remember at the age of seven asking my mother: *If I become a nun and a nurse can I get married? Or what about it if I become only a nurse?* The reason I remember this incident is because I can never forget the puzzled look on her face. Otherwise I don't remember the answer.

My first introduction to St. Francis of Assisi took place when a Redemptorist priest spoke of him in a homily during the devotions to Our Lady of Perpetual Help which all the children of our school attended each Tuesday. His words touched my heart. A few years later I found a practical vision of life in the Peace Prayer attributed to Francis. The contrast between the Peace Prayer, especially the words "not to be loved, but to love" and some of the songs I listened to on the Hit Parade, gave me a desire to give my heart to God and others in my daily living.

During high school days the words, "Let prayer and sacrifice be your great strength for they are invincible," as inscribed on our Grade Ten classroom chalk board, burned into my heart and guided me through my teen-age struggles. At that same time I also received a challenge in the words of Our Lady of Fatima: "So many souls go to hell because there is no one to pray for them."

After completing my education I began teaching elementary school children, work I loved. My prayer life was growing as I received the sacraments frequently and joined the Secular Franciscans. After three years of teaching I applied to join a religious community. At the last minute I realized I was not free enough so I changed my plans and continued teaching. Two years later I was soul-searching a commitment either to the religious life or marriage. I chose a community of teaching sisters that I knew well, but my commitment lasted a mere four months. This experience prepared me for my Poor Clare vocation. The Lord had spoken powerfully to me through the poem "The Hound Of Heaven" by Francis Thompson, my favorite quote being: "Ah fondest, blindest, weakest, I am He Whom Thou seekest!" (*Poems Vol. 1*, 1913 copyright USA, Charles Scribner's Sons). When I returned home I found that my spiritual life had deepened and as a result I had lost my taste for many of the attractions I had enjoyed before. My former postulant directress, who thought I still had a religious vocation, suggested that I pray for that desire. My prayer eventually did bear fruit and I was able to surrender unconditionally to God's will. Shortly after that moment of surrender a friend told me of her visit to a Poor Clare monastery in New Westminster, British Columbia. Her description of the peace and poverty of this recently founded monastery gave me a moment of peace that I had never experienced before. My agony in the garden had ceased, and my heart told me where I belonged.

I knew and loved St. Francis but I felt a stranger to St. Clare as at that time, 1955, I could not find much in print about her. That was to change when I entered the monastery on the Feast of St. Clare 1956. I was given Clare's letters to St. Agnes of Prague to read. I found her words speaking directly to my heart as if she were nearby. She was so loving and understanding of the heart of a young woman who was living so many centuries after her time. She has truly become my Sister and Mother as I imbibed and still imbibe the spirituality of loving surrender to Jesus under the devoted guidance of His Virgin Mother Mary.

I am most grateful to be able to share with St. Agnes of Prague and with all the generations of Poor Clares who have inherited and who are still sharing Saint Clare's magnificent Gospel charism in 2004 — 750 years after her death!

Sister Mary Clare McDonald, O.S.C.
Alexandria, Ontario, Canada

"Totally love Him who gave Himself totally for your love."   *3LAg 15b*

Late Have I Loved You

"Late have I loved you, O Beauty ever ancient, ever new, late have I loved you! You were within me, but I was outside and it was there that I searched for you." (*Confessions of St. Augustine*)

My journey to our monastery was a road of many twists and turns. I attended Catholic grade schools and from the third grade on, I felt a strong pull toward religious life. At 18, my family circumstances changed drastically when my father died suddenly of a massive heart attack and my mother was diagnosed with terminal cancer. As the oldest of five children, I accepted the family responsibilities thrust upon me while continuing my college education, working toward a teaching degree. My mother's condition required surgery, radiation and chemotherapy over a period of nine years. During this time, I felt religious life was not God's plan for me. I married and continued to care for my mother, along with my younger sisters and brother.

Shortly after my mother died, my husband decided that he did not want to have children. The Church annulled my marriage. By this time, my siblings were all on their own, and I began to reflect on religious life again. I had developed a habit of visiting Jesus in the Blessed Sacrament whenever I had the opportunity, after work and on weekends. I became involved with a lay community whose purpose was to foster spiritual growth. There was a new religious community being formed whose work was to provide the spiritual programs for this lay community. With my teaching background, I felt that God was calling me to this new religious community to work with their lay apostolate.

After a year and a half, I felt that religious life was not where God wanted me and I returned to lay life. I continued to be involved in my parish as a Lector, an Extraordinary Minister of Holy Communion and in spiritual programs. I was trying to stay open to God's plans for me and prayed for guidance. I decided not to return to teaching and I went back to school to become computer literate. I began to work in my parish office preparing the parish bulletin each week.

TOR Franciscan friars staffed our parish. One of the newly assigned priests had been in formation work within his province for quite a few years. After discussing my previous experience in religious life with him, he encouraged me to seek healing by speaking with a sister in an established religious community. He mentioned two possibilities, both friends of his, one who was in an active community and one who was cloistered. I chose the cloistered sister, telling him that "This is safe. I am not interested in cloistered life at all."

My first visit to Langhorne was a powerful experience for me in my heart and soul. I spoke with the formation directress and received the healing I needed. While praying in the monastery chapel, I felt the strength of God's call again to become a sister. I was afraid to even think about trying again. I told the directress my feelings and that I needed to step back to pray and reflect.

I returned for a week live-in experience and later for a month with the sisters. Both times I felt so much at home and very comfortable with the prayer schedule and the rhythm of the Poor Clare life. Once again, God gave me the grace to give away my worldly possessions to receive the spiritual blessings of religious life. I entered the Langhorne monastery in May of 1999 and made my First Profession on May 25, 2002. I continue to feel a deep sense of gratitude to God, the sisters here, and to the people who have been so instrumental in my journey to our monastery. The friar who encouraged me to come to Langhorne gave the homily during the Mass where I made my first profession. He traced my willingness to be open to the mystery and movement of God in my life. He also asked my friends and family to be attentive and respond to that same mystery and movement in their own lives. My prayer is that many women will listen to His call to our Poor Clare life and respond to his movement in their lives.

Sister Patricia Anne Coogan, O.S.C.
Langhorne, Pennsylvania

"Love God and Jesus, His Son...from the depths of your heart."   LEr 11a

The Story Of A Life

They have been happy and contented years, these forty years that I've spent in the Presence of Jesus.

As a young woman, I wanted a spousal relationship with Jesus Christ whom I wanted to love more than anyone else, and to whom I wanted to give my whole self. To dwell under the same roof with Him in the Holy Eucharist, and never to leave His side, was the great desire of my heart. I wanted to speak to Him often in the silent language of love during frequent periods of prayer. I wanted to do it all following in the spirit of that Saint of seraphic joy and simplicity — St. Francis of Assisi.

The life of a Poor Clare Sister is more than long periods of formal prayer. I live in a house with other consecrated women. As I relate to them on a daily basis — even an hourly basis — I have the opportunity to do as Jesus wishes when He tells His disciples to "love one another as I have loved you." For me that has taken the form of serving the Sisters as cook and of caring for those who are elderly and infirm.

The story of my perseverance as a Poor Clare Nun for so many years is a story of God's faithfulness to me. My life has not been an easy one; yet it's been a fulfilled one. I've given Jesus my mite, and He has multiplied it beyond measure. It's really true that He repays a hundredfold whatever you give to Him.

Having lived in the presence of Jesus all these years, it seems natural to me to look ahead to the time when I will see Him face to face in the eternal embrace of heaven. Yes, they've been good, these years in the Monastery of St. Clare on Nurrenbern Road; and the best is yet to come!

Sister M. Veronica, O.S.C.
Evansville, Indiana

"Place your mind before the mirror of eternity!"   *3LAg 12a*

Remembering the Call

The first stirrings of my vocation began as a teenager when I would accompany my dad to go fishing. We would go to a private place, and as I sat on a rock quietly for hours while waiting for a fish to bite, I was caught up in the meaning of life. The quiet and beauty that surrounded me eventually drew me to heavenly realities and to the possibility of the cloistered life. I desired to live a life that focused on prayer and the needs of the world. My name being "Therese Marie," I also drew a lot of inspiration from the autobiography of St. Therese, *Story of a Soul*. As much as I admired the Carmelite vocation, circumstances led me to join a Poor Clare Monastery. I knew in my heart that this is where God was calling me.

I am still a Poor Clare today and hope to be until I draw my last breath because I promised to do so as I took my vows of Poverty, Chastity, Obedience and Enclosure many years ago. I love my God, my vocation, my particular community (each sister is close to my heart), and I have a deep desire to lift up to God the needs of the entire world and to evangelize through my life of prayer.

We are praying that many women will follow in the footsteps of St. Clare in response to the call of Jesus.

Sister Therese Marie Lacroix, O.S.C.
Andover, Massachusetts

"Place your soul in the brilliance of glory!"   *3LAg 12b*

Joy Through Suffering

Before coming to the Monastery, I desired very much a calling to the contemplative life. Deep in my soul I knew God doesn't change. I felt very secure in this knowledge and wanted to entrust my whole life to this Being. I didn't know if God wanted me to be a nun or not, but I sure wanted it! I must admit I did not think I was qualified for this life and I didn't have confidence in myself. I didn't think a monastery would accept me.

I went to daily Mass and worked for the youth in our parish. I sang in the choir and belonged to the Legion of Mary. Sometimes I acted in the church plays. In this activity my health was restored and I became bright and happy. Yet in all this I wanted to offer my whole life to God as a nun. I sought out more and more times for private prayer where I could be alone with God. These were very precious moments for me.

I started going to the Carmelite Monastery in our region as a candidate. I was terribly disappointed when they asked me to look into other places before deciding to enter. I wanted to enter right away. At this time big problems started coming up at work, in relationships with my family and friends. Just "to be" became very painful, heavy and a burden. I was confused by these problems and brokenhearted. I decided to take a vacation to Jeju Island. A Sister in my parish once told me "go to St. Clare's Monastery on Jeju." To this day that Sister and I don't know why she said that, but she just spontaneously said this to me. I'm sure it was the Holy Spirit. Looking back I see God had prepared me for this place.

My first retreat at St. Clare's Monastery was wonderful with many graces being given me. My heart was healed and I was able to forgive. I was converted. My relationships were healed and restored to their former ways. Through the Word of God I gained new life and new courage. My heart was at peace and I felt St. Clare guiding me. When I went home I could not forget this monastery so I didn't go to Carmel anymore. I started pestering Jesus at prayer to let me enter the Monastery on Jeju. I felt deeply the mystery of God in all that I had experienced especially how all the problems I knew I couldn't solve were now solved without me doing anything.

Finally I entered the Monastery. This was such a surprising and wonderful gift for me after wanting so much to become a Poor Clare. I knew God who had called me and led me all along had put all things in order for me. I felt God's love so very much with me. I was reborn. What I desired now I possessed. I have discovered in living this life that I must respond to my calling anew each day. Many times I'm tempted to become very selfish and unable to die to my false self. At those times I feel St. Clare helping me especially through her writings. I hear her whisper to me: "Be poor, just be poor." This sets me free and gives me a deep joy.

I have walked through a tunnel of pain and death and came out walking with Jesus in a resurrected life. Now all suffering, joy, all things in creation...all are good. All things are Christ's.

Sister Magdelena Hong, O.S.C.
Jeju Island, Korea

"You always remember your resolution and be conscious of your beginning."
2LAg 11a

My Vocation Call

"But now, thus says the Lord, who created you, O Jacob, and formed you, O Israel: Fear not for I have redeemed you; I have called you by name; are you mine." (Isaiah 43:1) "The Lord called me from birth, from my mother's womb He gave me my name." (Isaiah. 49:1)

These two passages from Isaiah seem to best describe my birth and my Call. I was born December 9, 1929. At Baptism the next day I was given my name Mary Ellen. I was born into a good Catholic family. I had an uncle who was a Benedictine Brother, and an aunt, Sister Mary Paschal, a Poor Clare Nun here in Evansville. The story goes that I was only about four months old when I was brought down to visit her. While I was a very happy child and had lots of fun, I was also very pious; loving spiritual things, religious songs, holy cards, etc., anything pertaining to Jesus and the saints. I belonged to Jesus in a very special way from my birth and the desire to be His grew with each breath I took. As soon as I knew about being a nun, being a spouse of Christ, belonging to Jesus, I desired it.

Being born at the time of the Depression, money was scarce. Having read that nuns had to pay a dowry worried me. There were five boys and three girls to feed and clothe (2 brothers died in infancy). So I worked; I prayed and I hoped...and I found out that Poor Clare Sisters did not have to have a dowry.

Since I was going to be a Poor Clare nun, I wanted to go to the Ferdinand Academy. My parents felt they couldn't afford my going but we arranged that I could work my way through and they made sacrifices for me. It was a great experience of my first being away from home.

In August, after my freshman year, I came to Evansville to plead with the abbess to let me come. "No, you're still too young." In the meantime I had to get a letter of recommendation from my pastor and he was not ready to give it to me. He wanted me to be Benedictine because they needed teachers. Finally I convinced him and he gave me the letter I needed. In October, the abbess wrote to my parents saying I could come anytime. When I told my friends, they said, "Oh, but how can you go before Christmas and leave all your brothers and sisters?" I told them I wanted to be there for Christmas. They convinced me to stay at least until Thanksgiving, which I did, and they had a nice farewell party for me. That Thanksgiving was our last family dinner together, all ten of us, or at least I thought so at the time. Finally we were on our way. It was a cold, dreary day in November and the trip was like a funeral procession. I was the first of eight children to leave home at age 14, going on 15, and I was like a mother to the five younger ones. When we arrived at 2:00 the sisters were going to confession until, at 4:00, they rang the bell. All the sisters gathered in the hall and we went over to the enclosure door. All of a sudden my mother began sobbing. Thank God, my Grandma (her mother) was there and she said, "Remember Loretta. It's not like she's dead. You can write to her and visit her." Grandma knew what it was like when her own daughter, Sister Mary Paschal, left home. We said our final farewells. I was delighted but also sad and scared. I could just picture them, heartbroken, returning to their homes.

My fervor really grew as I finally realized I would soon wear a wedding dress and be called by a new name. I would be one step closer to being Christ's bride forever. As my clothing day came I felt I could hardly contain myself. When Father at the grate said, "You will no longer be called Mary Ellen Blandford but Sister Mary Martha of the Holy Face," I was overwhelmed.

My First Profession was on Thursday, March 13. Since it was a weekday none of my family could come. It was a workday and a school day, and in those days no one could take off. The Sisters made an exception and I was allowed to visit my Aunt, Sister Mary Paschal, in the infirmary. To be honest, it felt very strange but it was a concession and I was grateful.

The day I had been waiting for all my life finally came. At last I was to become **His** forever. That day I will never forget. I felt my heart would burst with joy! There were two of us that bright, cold December day: Sister Mary Bernardine and myself. It was December 13, 1950, a Marian Year. Father Eligius Weir, O.F.M. celebrated the Eucharist and conducted the ceremony. It was all so heavenly I felt like I was in ecstasy. After all was over, we went to the parlor. My uncle, Brother James, O.S.B., said to me, "Sister, now you have one more day more beautiful, more special even than today." I looked at him with questions in my eyes. He said to me, "The day of your death." At that time I was not too far advanced in spirituality, and this seemed strange to me. You should have seen the look on my dad's face! That whole day was one of the most beautiful days of my life and the memory of those six years in the Novitiate will remain with me and inspire me and bless me until I meet my beloved Spouse in heaven.

With all you have just read, my vocation story has really just begun. It is not, in fact, a matter of living happily ever after. As St. Paul writes, "even now I find my joy in the sufferings I endure for you. In my own flesh I fill up what is lacking in the sufferings of Christ for the sake of His body, the Church." (Colossians 1:24). Yet for myself I have found the joys outweigh the sorrows, the temptations, and the trials of Poor Clare community living. The very fact that, as I have often said and fully believe, "I belong to Him and He belongs to me" cannot be fully fathomed.

If I had to do it all over again, would I make the same choices? Yes!

Through my union with Jesus and in the enclosure of my heart, I am called to embrace every human being, every human situation and bring every instant of my life into the Presence of my loving Triune God!

Sister Mary Martha Blandford, O.S.C.
Evansville, Indiana

"As a poor virgin, embrace the poor Christ."   2LAg 18

God's Leading

From my early youth, I had always desired to become a religious sister, but it was not actually realized until my late 30s.

Having been taught by religious sisters, I came to realize that each had her own personal characteristics. Some were especially jovial and fun to be with, others were more quiet, caring and compassionate. Some were teachers and superiors whom I greatly admired and who encouraged me, and others possessed different ways that were challenges for growth. Religious life was not unknown to my family — a few had entered in previous generations. I fondly remember meeting our great aunt on family visits. In those days, even active religious lived very much a monastic lifestyle...when they would occasionally be seen on the streets in "two" or "three" as they went about doing their errands.

The desire to become a religious was always and constantly a part of me — more than my consideration of ever being married or having a family, though I highly valued and treasured family life! I wanted to give my life to God more fully within the church, even if it meant in a "hidden" way. From my earliest childhood, I would pray for the missionaries and people living in the Third World, in Africa, for example. To me, it made the world seem so much smaller ... more "global" in scope ... our connection to one another!

A contemplative community of religious sisters who were also located in our city also positively influenced me. It was very common, almost routine, that as my father drove the whole family back home from Sunday Mass, we would stop at their chapel along the way to pay a brief visit to the Blessed Sacrament. Although I yearned to come here more often, I could not do so as we lived several miles away. However, during my working years I would often stop in to chat with Jesus many, many times and to pray for those in need. I always felt our city was particularly blessed to have this Chapel of Perpetual Adoration open day and night, during a time in church history when most parishes locked their doors after Mass.

I thank God also for growing up during the era of the Second Vatican Council that permitted more participation of the laity and women in the church, for I enjoyed lectoring and cantoring, participating in parish social activities and experiencing the bondedness of parish family life. This enabled me to keep the seed of religious vocation alive and active in some small way during my work years.

Although I was always very grateful for the presence of religious communities in my life, somehow I felt that God was not calling me as yet to enter any but rather I was to keep the "kernel" of Africa alive, though I did not know what this meant. I had never envisioned myself ever going to Africa and yet, much to my surprise, this was to be God's way of leading me to the community he had in mind, that of the Poor Clares!

It came in a roundabout way when I had returned to college after 15 wonderful, challenging, exciting and very busy years of work, to obtain a bachelor's degree in my field. One Sunday morning at the local church I was attending, a fund drive was being conducted by a Franciscan missionary sister whose community's apostolate was dedicated to ministering to the peoples of Africa. As she spoke, I could feel the deep, burning desire within my heart to reach out to these people who had long been part of my prayer and spiritual growth. In our brief sharing after Mass, I was asked to look into a vocation with them. In our subsequent correspondences, I asked if I could go to Africa to serve as a "lay missionary" among their Sisters. And so to Africa I went.

During my initial months there, I was graced with an opportunity to make a directed retreat, and it was during this time of prayer that I sensed God calling me back to the States to consider the Poor Clare life. Thus with deep trust in God's leading my life, I walked forward with my hand clasped in God's. My journey toward a contemplative life was begun and has continued to unfold over these past ten years. What very graced and joyful memories of entering, making Simple Profession and Solemn Profession with this community!

I pray that God will grant you His grace, vision and perseverance for your life as you journey with Him.

Sister M. Jean Therese Rossignol, O.S.C.
Langhorne, Pennsylvania

"Let us pray to God for one another."   *LEr 17a*

Jesus Speaks to Children's Hearts

I always wanted to be a nun. I knew in my heart that Jesus wanted me to be His alone. My parents took us children to Mass every day and from there I drew my strength. I listened to the readings as if they were meant for me and I practiced living them every day. In the evening we said the rosary and the Legion of Mary prayers and I talked to our Lady at that time. After school every day I made a visit to Jesus in the Blessed Sacrament, and I told Him all about the day, my joys and my troubles, and asked Him for help. I always prayed for others, especially for my family, friends and priests. I was always telling Jesus I loved Him and listening to His love for me. Once a month we went to the Secular Franciscans' meeting and at the age of fourteen, I joined the Franciscans.

This lifestyle naturally flowed into a religious vocation. At our evening prayers we had always prayed "for vocations in the family," and I had always hoped that I would be an answer to that prayer. We had also thanked God during those prayers "for my faith"; I for many years had been thanking Him for my "face!"

It came to pass that one day at an afternoon visit of the Secular Franciscans to Westminster Abbey, a gentleman asked us if we'd ever met the Poor Clares nearby. I was ready for the actual call of God to come into my heart as I walked through the door of the Poor Clare monastery. I knew immediately that this was the place for me to live with Jesus forever.

When I was younger I had known only about active sisters, so I had decided to become a White Sister, a missionary to Africa. Then I read the *Story of a Soul*, the autobiography of St. Therese of Lisieux, the Little Flower, a Carmelite nun in France at the end of the 19th century. She had spoken of just being with Jesus and loving Him and letting him do whatever He liked with us, like a ball a child can pick up and play with or put down and leave alone whenever he wanted. That was the life I wanted.

I had not known of any actual monasteries that lived this contemplative life until I met the Poor Clares. They were poor and lived for God alone, hidden away, separated from others, always listening to Jesus and loving Him, like Mary at Jesus' feet. I couldn't yet leave my dear family so I continued to attend UBC taking Honours in Classics. One day I suddenly knew I could leave and become a nun.

I had been visiting the Poor Clares on weekends; now I applied to enter. On March 25th, 1973, the Solemnity of the Annunciation, I entered. It was hard to leave my family but the thought of belonging to Jesus made it possible. After six months I became a novice on October 1st and took the name "Sister Marie Therese (Murphy) of the Child Jesus." My Greek professor did the necessary work to get my B.A. degree for me; I had left so suddenly with no concern for leaving behind my degree.

On October 1, 1975, I made my first vows and on December 12, 1978, my solemn vows. During the Great Julilee of the year 2000, I celebrated my silver jubilee and relived my courtship and marriage with Jesus. To do every little thing with Him and for Him is the heart of my life and I thank Him for making me His.

Sister Marie Therese (Murphy) of the Child Jesus, O.S.C.
Mission, B.C., Canada

"...by carrying each other's burden of charity...we will easily fulfill the law of Christ."   *LEr 17b*

The Mystery of My Life

From the beginning of my life to the end, my life is one of living in God's mercy. This grace of mercy is the biggest and most important factor in my calling as a Poor Clare.

Before I even considered knocking on the monastery door, my heart was filled to the brim with plans for my own future. Although my friends spoke to me about a religious vocation, their words could not penetrate my heart. I was deaf to them.

One day I happened to see a movie about the life of St. Francis of Assisi. A seed was dropped into my heart. Through Francis, I met Clare. These two saints living the Gospel life stirred in my heart a great desire to follow their example. They became my models in trying to live the high ideals of Gospel perfection. That is when I saw in myself the tendency to see life as a high ideal. There was one problem. My high ideals and reality were far apart.

Gradually I was able to see my real self. I had much darkness inside me and I was a very weak person. To cover up this truth, I had to put on armor to make me strong. I became very critical of others. I was judgmental and hard, walking down a narrow path of perfection — or so I thought. Still in all of this I felt God leading along another road. At prayer I would rest in God and know God was waiting for me.

My greatest sorrow was when my elder sister died suddenly. She had been included in my rejection and criticisms. She had needed me to listen to her in her hardships and sufferings. When she died my greatest pain was in realizing I had not loved her. Here I was living in the warmth of God's love and light; yet I could not translate this to my outward world. I was only living in my head. I was a failure as a Christian. How could I live this life? It would be better to leave. My heart was so pained I didn't know how I could bear it. And yet in all this God did come to console me. I felt God with me, accepting my pained heart.

Three years after my sister's death and greatest sorrow, I received my greatest joy. My mother had died when I was a baby. After her death I became very ill. I was taken to many doctors but they couldn't help me. Lastly I was taken to a Maryknoll sister-doctor in Pusan. She treated me for sometime but saw I wasn't responding so she baptized me thinking I was dying. She gave me the name Clara after her friend. I was one year old at this time. Several years ago through letters I was reunited with this sister. She is Sr. Gilmary at Maryknoll, New York. She told me my coming back to life after being so close to death was a profound experience for her. In my re-birth, she felt deeply the saving power of God and God's miracle. She experienced

God's presence through my life. When she told me this several years ago, I discovered a deep, deep joy and meaning in my life and in all of life. I saw how precious I was and how God had preserved me for this life. My life is now a song of praise and thanksgiving to God who heals the brokenhearted and renews us each day.

I still have moments of darkness mixed with light but now I understand myself better. From my experience I can go out to others in their trials and give them courage. When I come to die, I want to be able to say like our Mother Clare, "May you be blessed, O Lord. You who have created my soul...."

Sister Clara Lee, O.S.C.
Jeju Island, Korea

"Happy indeed is she to whom it is given to share in this sacred banquet so that she might cling with all her heart to Him."   *4LAg 9*

The Monastery

This place would be a gate
that easily swings in;
a simple gate, fine wood, highly polished and smooth,
a silent gate that only whispers when it is swung,
    a gate that leads to a garden of lovely flowers,
                    all varieties,
               beautiful colors,
          lovely fragrances,
each different, but none competing, none overpowering,
each yielding and blending with the others.

All turned toward the sun, all responding to the same rain and wind
and snow, each sharing the same tribulations, all accepting what is,
none hiding from what all must share.

All sensitive to the need to root out any weeds that come, but no
one afraid of the thorns of another.

This garden would be visited by others who came to enjoy the
beauty and the sweetness, to gain strength and courage for their
own journey. But the flowers have no voice so it is by their lives
that the message is given:

    a message of peace, of harmony, of beauty and simplicity,
        of confidence on God to send the sun and the rain,
            to preserve them from scavengers or enemies.

Part 2: I'm His...From Forever

They wait and turn toward the sun and listen to the wind and sometimes wake to watch the stars in silence, to wonder and give praise...
Until that day when they will be picked by the Hand of God
and be caught up to the sky to shine there with the stars.

Sister Barbara Borst, O.S.C.
Duncan, B.C., Canada

*"And transform your entire being into the image of the Godhead Itself
through contemplation."* 3LAg 13b

The Evangelical Life of Saint Clare

Her Spiritual Quest

A few months after the death of Clare, Pope Innocent IV, who had approved the Rule of Clare, inaugurated the process of Clare's canonization as a saint to be celebrated in the Roman Church. The first step in the process was an official interview, under oath, of thirteen sisters who had lived with Clare at San Damiano. We have their stories. It is interesting to note that many of these stories about Clare go back to the beginning of her vocation. This is oral history that can often give a truer perspective on the important features of a person's life than the more formal canonical documents.

Pacifica was the first sister to give her testimony about Clare. Pacifica's family home was across the Piazza of San Rufino from that of Clare. Ortulana, Clare's mother, took Pacifica as a companion when she went on pilgrimage to the Holy Land in 1192 shortly before Clare's birth. From Pacifica we learn that Clare began her spiritual quest while she was quite young and that there was a group of girls and women who shared with one another their enthusiasm for following Christ. Prayer, fasting and almsgiving were part of her life even before she began meeting with Francis and Philip.

Part 2: I'm His...From Forever

Clare was eighteen when she ran away from home in the dead of night to meet Francis and his companions at the little chapel of Our Lady of the Angels on the plain below Assisi. That her family was against her determination to forge a new religious path did not deter her. She spurned both the vocation of marriage and that of traditional religious life. Clare gave the first fruits of her young life without reserve and gave herself in confidence that God who inspired her vocation would see it faithfully to full fruition....

Ordinary Women Living an Extraordinary Life With Christ

*Poor Clare Sisters living religious life
for 50 to 76 years!*

Mary, My Mother

I was born of very pious parents who raised us kids to be good Catholics. My mother came from Lithuania at 12 years of age with her parents and settled in West Hazleton, Pennsylvania. My father worked in the coal mines for 30 years and developed the black lung condition. For the last seven years of his life, he was the sacristan for our parish church.

I was very sickly when I was born in 1909, a "yellow baby." It was doubtful whether I would survive. My holy mother bundled up her newborn and carried me through the Pennsylvania winter weather to the neighborhood church and placed me on the Blessed Virgin's altar. She dedicated me to her and asked her to watch over me and to give me health.

When I was a young girl our parish had a Mission, and the preacher encouraged the young folks to think about religious life. I felt inspired by God to respond to this call, and so I approached our parish priest. My dear friend Ann also felt called, so together we applied to the Sisters of St. Casimir. I was told to wait because I was too young and had not finished elementary school, but my friend and I were not about to be separated. Ann wrote a letter to the foundress of the community, Mother Maria Kaupas, S.S.C., in words similar to these:

Dear Mother General: Helen and I have been pals since our childhood days and we would like to consecrate our lives to God at the same time. May she please come? *Ann*

So it came to pass, at the age of fourteen, my friend Ann and I entered the community in August 1923.

Although my friend had to leave due to ill health, I remained and was professed. I taught school and later trained as a registered nurse. All during this time I had a desire for a greater life of prayer, but I didn't know how this was to come about.

It was through the help of my spiritual director that the way became clear for me to act. I was accepted by the Poor Clares of New Orleans, and transferred on October 12, 1950. During my trip to New Orleans from Chicago, we shared the train with the Notre Dame football team. The coach graciously bought dinner for me and my companion, a treat that we enjoyed very much indeed.

I have now been a professed religious over 75 years, and the Blessed Mother continues to watch over me as my mother asked more than 95 years ago.

If I were giving advice to someone considering religious life today, I would say: Pray to the Holy Spirit, and place your trust in Mary. Even though you can't see how things will turn out, with God everything is always for the best.

Sister Marie Lapinskas, O.S.C.
New Orleans, Louisiana

"What you hold, may you always hold; What you do, may you always do and never abandon. 2LAg 11b

God's Providential Care

My parents, Mary Elizabeth and Francis Joseph Hutfless, waited seven years for me, Mary Frances, their first and only child, to be conceived. I was born six months after my father died. He had rheumatism, which left him unable to turn himself in bed; my mother took care of him. Father Edward Flanagan of Boys Town fame was the assistant pastor of St. Patrick's Parish and he came every day for a month to visit my father before he died. He also baptized me.

The Extern Poor Clare Sisters used to come with the horse and buggy in our neighborhood to beg for whatever supplies the people would give them. I used to go around saying, "I'm going to be a little Sister of the Poor." My mother had to work so she took me to St. Joseph Academy for the school year but I was with her in the summer with our relatives. I lived with my aunt when mother worked in Montana and I began to go to Mass every day especially during Lent and attended Catholic school there. I felt very comfortable with the Blessed Virgin Mary Sisters; they were very patient with me. I noticed how good they were to the poor Mexican people who worked there too. When I began the eighth grade Mother Divine Shepherd wrote to my mother to invite me to come back to St. Joseph's Academy, which I did. I stayed for another year and took a commercial course and ancient history. Some of the girls were leaving to enter religious communities at that time. One day I picked up a magazine that talked about sisters who worked with the lepers in Louisiana and I thought that maybe I could help God's suffering ones. Some of the girls entered the Poor Clare Community in Evansville, Indiana. I remembered my early association with Poor Clares and my director, Father Cassilly, S.J. said that he would help me enter the Omaha Poor Clare community. Two of us wanted to enter so I entered on the Feast of Corpus Christi, June 19, 1930. I had just turned sixteen. Since we had a Sister Mary Francis, I received the name Mary Celine, after the Poor Clare Sister Marie Celine who lived at the same time as St. Therese "the Little Flower" and who died in the odor of sanctity in France.

When I entered so many persons wondered how my mother was able to consent to her only child entering a cloistered community! The day I entered mother and some relatives and friends came with us. Mother was crying and I asked her why. She said that they were tears of gratitude. She was so grateful to God that he called me to be His bride. I was happy in my religious vocation but the many changes after Vatican II were a great challenge for me.

Sister Mary Celine Hutfless, O.S.C.
Omaha, Nebraska

"But with swift pace, light step, unswerving feet so that even your steps stir up no dust."   *21LAg 12*

Everlasting Love

Our Franciscan footprints throughout the world follow pathways of the Holy Gospel and Jesus our Brother is the leader.

When I was eight years old, my father was asked directions from a group of young men dressed in brown and wearing sandals. My mind immediately took a photograph that would never fade. I sensed kindness and joy!

Four years later my mother found Saint Clare's Chapel in Belfast, Ireland. We listened to the Sisters chanting prayers that Sunday. I remember her words: "Jesus is really here," a memory of voices and prayerful sounds, also to remain always in the background of my mind.

Nevertheless new exciting sounds became my priority, sounds of ice skaters in Central Park, waves of the ocean in summer time, my family on Thanksgiving Day, friends and children's laughter; all part of happy teenage years.

One Christmas shopping day right in the heart of the Big Apple my sister suggested a place to slow down. It was "Divine Providence." My footprints would soon be walking the Franciscan-Clarian pathways. The atmosphere of peace that we found in the Church of Saint Francis of

Assisi brought back past memories and the words "Jesus is really here."

The words of Jeremiah also would follow my footprints, whispering the Holy Spirit's message: "I have loved you with an everlasting love, so I am constant in my affection for you" (Jeremiah 31:3). I was now twenty-four, giving my affections to the transient.

My religious journey began the day the Poor Clares in the Bronx, New York, received me. Five years later a new foundation was made in Brazil. Nine other Sisters and I left the asphalt streets of New York to bring the Franciscan-Clarian spirituality to the land of the Holy Cross for twenty-four years.

Saint Clare remained always in Assisi in her first foundation at San Damiano. Eight hundred years have gone into eternity. Clare's silent life of love continues to speak, drawing young women to stop and listen. Your name may be on an invitation to follow this form of Life! Saint Clare's answer was "yes."

My seventy years of life have many footprints. I walked the way of the Gospels of Jesus, and our Holy Mother Clare gives us a safe road to travel, her "form of life."

"Always be lovers of God, of your soul and of the souls of all your Sisters and may you be always eager to observe what you have promised the Lord." Words of Saint Clare. (BCl 14).

Sister Lucy Houston, O.S.C.
New Rochelle, New York

"May you go forward securely, joyfully and swiftly on the path of prudent happiness."
2LAg 13

An Illness Plus a Book

Our parish priest was great for recruiting vocations. Six boys became priests, two became brothers and many girls entered religious life. When preparing to receive First Holy Communion he suggested we pray that Jesus call us to be His bride. This was a great attraction for a six-year-old. My only sister did enter religious life at sixteen years of age when I was eight. My mother took me along when my sister went to enter and I missed two days of school. My teacher was very displeased at my missing school, so she did not pass me into the next grade. I was **mad**!

At eleven I became very sick with pleurisy and double pneumonia and was anointed. A Canadian neighbor's boy died of it. The whole parish was praying for me. During that illness the life of St. Therese was read to me, as she was becoming very popular at the time. What most affected me was that she never left her monastery but through prayer saved souls throughout the world. Before this I had wanted to enter with my sister's community, but I did not tell anyone. I also felt called to go and care for lepers or to go to China, as a boy from our parish became a foreign missionary priest and worked in China. Yet I did not feel called to be a Carmelite like St. Therese.

My mother took subscriptions for the *Franciscan Review*, and when visiting my aunt in Montreal, I took the subscriptions to the monastery and there met Fr. Thomas, O.F.M., who had just returned from a trip to Victoria, B.C., and had visited the monastery of the Poor Clares. Something clicked in me at the time when he told me about them. Father asked me to write them but I hesitated doing so. At last I did send an offering asking them to pray I would pass my exams which I did, even coming in second with honors. I was not a brilliant student so it was a surprise to everyone. The CWL gave a gift to the two highest grades so I received a statue of St. Therese which was their gift that year.

With a thank-you note and assurance of prayers for me from the Poor Clares was a leaflet telling briefly about their life and their daily schedule. I kept reading it and being more and more drawn to live a life of prayer and to help souls get to know Jesus' great love for them. It kept nagging at me.

At the end of my first year of high school, my dad was bedridden for ten months so I stopped school near the end of the term to help care for him as I was the only one at home with my mother. The day before he died, as I was sitting beside him, he asked me what I planned on doing. He was the first one I told about wanting to enter the Poor

Clares. That did not matter to me. He was happy for he had a great love for religious who dedicated their lives to Jesus and helped save souls.

After he died, my mother and I moved to Kingston, where I attended Notre Dame Academy. I gradually got friendly with three girls. At the end of the term all three of us were planning on entering, unknown to each other, and each in a different community. One died as a novice, the other three of us are still living at the age of 87 and communicating by mail in different parts of Canada.

My uncle and guardian paid my fare to Victoria from Montreal, which was a four-day journey across Canada. I traveled with two other girls. Especially interesting were the Rockies. We arrived on the feast of St. Clare in 1933. After supper we were ushered to our rooms as it was said we needed extra sleep after our long journey.

It was interesting to learn about and live our Poor Clare life and to get to know and love Jesus who was to be our special Spouse. One of the challenges was trying to recognize each sister in their long, patched habit and hand-made sandals fashioned with pieces of carpet. Work was assigned to each one: sacristy, sewing, cooking and washing clothes by hand as we did not have a washing machine at that time. Clothes were put on the lawn to bleach.

One year we were given a cord of wood in three-foot lengths that had to be sawn individually. Most sisters had never sawed wood in their lives. The house was heated with wood that had to be brought in each day. This was "fun" even in bad weather.

Working in the garden was new to most of us who had no experience in that area. We had to make sure it was a weed we were pulling up and not a precious flower. We climbed ladders to pick fruit, holding them in gunnysack aprons and making sure a bee was not feasting in a pear ready to sting us. Making altar breads without modern equipment was also quite a feat.

After sixteen years I was chosen to go on to our new foundation in the Archdiocese of Vancouver. That was something! We lived in a tiny cottage, and I missed the exercise of running up and down three flights of stairs many times a day. Twelve years later our monastery was built in the beautiful Fraser Valley on a hill overlooking the Fraser River. This enabled us to see, year-round, snowcapped Mount Baker in the United States to the south. East of us is Hatzic Lake and Island, and from our vantage point we are able to see the Cheam Range sixty miles away, also snowcapped year-round. We never cease raving at the fantastic sunrises we experience.

A grace-filled experience in our community was caring for the youngest Sister who came to the foundation and was diagnosed with an inoperable brain tumor. We took care of her at home for nine months. What a beautiful experience for all of us! The day before Sister Mary Angela died, a newly-married bride came and left her bridal bouquet to be put in chapel as a token of gratitude. We took it to Sister Mary Angela, who died holding it in her hands. Sister Mary Angela's spirituality was very bridal, and she was a sister who had a very great insight and love for Jesus as her Spouse. What a joy for us all in the midst of our sorrow!

As Sister Mary Agnes was dying six months later, I had an appointment to see a hearing specialist. I had waited three months for it. I was told to go though I did not want to, as Sister Mary Agnes looked as if she would not live through the day. So I went to her asking her to "go" before I left or wait till I was back because I wanted to be with her when her Spouse took her to His everlasting embrace. Then I left to get ready for my appointment and heard the bell calling the community to Sister Mary Agnes' bedside as she was beginning to breathe her last. It was an everlasting joy for me, because I had cared for her the last years of her life. Indeed the Lord is good.

Seventy years later my heart continues to be full of gratitude for the call the Lord gave me to follow Him as a Poor Clare. With all my heart and soul I now prepare to follow

Him into His heavenly home and my great homecoming!
"My soul is longing and yearning for the courts of the
Lord!" (Psalm 84:2).

Sister Mary Barbara Collins, O.S.C.
Mission, B.C., Canada

*"Not believing anything, not agreeing with anything that would dissuade you
from this resolution or that would place a stumbling block for you on the way."*
2LAg 14a

God's Surprising Plans

I was born the 10th child in a family of 11 in Adrian, Minnesota, in 1918. My Mom was 40 years old when I was born, I often wondered if she was weary of one more child — yet I was never made to feel that way. Even as a young child I always said I would be a sister. My sister Lori and I often played "school" and I was Sister Bernadine!

The first 18 years of my life were spent on a farm and we worked hard; I learned the dignity of work at an early age. Lori and I never had trouble dividing our daily tasks. I always wanted to be the one to bring the cattle home for milking and I hoped they were be at the far end of the pasture as I had a list of hymns I wanted to sing. "Jesus, Jesus come to me"; and "Oh Lord, I am not worthy" were the ones I began with and there were four or five more! It was a disappointment to me when I got close to home; perhaps that was the beginning of my contemplative life.

I entered the Sisters of St. Francis in Rochester, Minnesota on August 18, 1936. As a professed sister of 64 years my heart is full of gratitude to the God who has directed my journey of many surprises. Jeremiah 29:11-15 has had a special significance in my life for God's way was not always my way. As I made my profession of vows on August 15, 1939, as a Sister of St. Francis I felt deep in my heart this was my life's commitment. Surprise! The Lord had other plans.

I spent 32 years as a happy Franciscan making a home for teaching sisters and as a supervisor of food service in several of our hospitals. In 1967 when renewal and many changes were happening in religious life, four of us sisters of St. Francis spent six weeks of prayer at the monastery in Bloomington, Minnesota, for the success of this renewal in our Congregation. It was a tremendous experience. The Lord was showing me again "I know my plans for you."

The following year at the suggestion of Sister Anne, a Poor Clare in Bloomington, I requested a year's sabbatical to spend at the monastery. What a gift! Somehow the quiet yearnings of my heart for more quiet and prayer were answered. Before my year of prayer was over I knew I was being called to this contemplative way of life. Again, after much discernment and advice, especially from Sister Anne and Sister Emmanuel from Rochester, I requested a transfer from my Franciscan community to the Poor Clare community. It was not an easy decision as I loved my sisters in Rochester dearly; and I visit them whenever I can. I received the permission from Rome, and on August 6, 1971, I made solemn vows as a Poor Clare. I spent nearly 20 years in Bloomington. In 1990 again I heard the Lord say: "I know my plans for you." I felt called to join three other sisters of St. Clare, at the request of Bishop Ken

Untener, who wanted to begin a foundation in Saginaw, Michigan.

We moved to Saginaw, October 15, 1991, and for my aging years this has been/is pure gift! I truly have the time, the space and the quiet my soul so longs for. As my steps get slower, my capacity for work is more limited. I am supremely happy, and my favorite Psalms at this time are: "My soul is thirsting for You, my God; when shall I see You face to face?" (Psalm 41) and "As a deer longs for running streams so my soul longs for You, my God."

Sister Bernardone Reining, O.S.C.
Saginaw, Michigan

"So that you may offer your vows to the Most High in the pursuit of that perfection to which the Spirit of the Lord has called you."   *2LAg 14b*

Another Woman's Hope Chest

I was the first of five girls born to Russian immigrants who settled in the newly developed Kooteney Valley in British Columbia. My father, in fleeing conscription in the Russian Army, found employment on the team constructing the railroad which opened up the West, and after several years was able to bring his Russian bride of only a few days to Canada. Speaking Russian at home and English in school, I developed the skills to bridge barriers, which would be my legacy throughout my life. Early days were spent among this close-knit family and friends whose Russian Orthodox faith kept them firmly rooted around the Church and its values of faithfulness, loyalty, honesty and hard work. Even today at the age of 93, these deeply rooted values are reflected in my relationships with others and with God.

Struggling through the Great Depression also influenced me, finding me employed in various occupations so as to support myself and to be of assistance to my family. My one-year experience of teaching in a multiple grade, one-room schoolhouse enabled me to save enough money to attend nursing school and later to become an instructor myself. Throughout these formative years, I remained faithful to my religious values, recognizing that my own strong will and feistiness were in need of the Lord's guidance and direction. But there was no definitive movement toward religious life or marriage.

In my late twenties, well established in my nursing career, my friendship with a long-time friend, Simonne, was to open up a new avenue for me. Visiting for a weekend to discuss plans for Simonne's upcoming wedding, we were exploring her hope chest, sorting through the lovely items that were soon to grace her new home. At the bottom of the chest, Simonne drew out some papers which she declared were "no longer needed" as her journey was leading in a new direction. Inquiring what they were, I discovered application forms for a Poor Clare community. "Give them to me," I replied (on what impulse I still cannot fully decipher) and that evening I filled out the form and mailed it to the community.

A few short weeks later, having left my cigarettes and lighter with the cab driver, I mounted the steps to the Monastery door and began my lifetime commitment to God as Sister Louise Belecky, a poor Sister of St. Clare.

Sister Louise Belecky, O.S.C.
Duncan, B.C., Canada

"If you weep with Him, you shall rejoice with Him."   2LAg 21 b

A True Little Story for the Young in Heart

(St. Clare of Assisi)

This dear little story is as true as can be,
It happened in Italy, in old Assisi.
It is 800 years now, that St. Clare took her flight…
To heaven, in glory immortal and bright.
She was very old then, about sixty, I think;
And her life of penance had passed by in a wink.
Clare was quite young though, when she first heard the call,
The Ideal of St. Francis… "My God and my All."

Their lives were so simple and easily told,
But the richness and beauty only angels behold.
St. Francis had taken quite a mystical view,
And embraced Lady Poverty in a way that was new.
Stripped of all his possessions save tunic and cord,
He followed barefooted his Master and Lord.
His mendicant Friars were most holy too,
And preached so sublimely, their words rang out true.

The Order of Poor Ladies in ideal the same,
Prayed hard and did penance, and hid far from fame.
Clare dwelt at St. Damiano with nuns not a few;
and daily her virtue and charity grew.

The people admired such ardor and zeal,
And time has not dimmed it or made it less real.
Their lives told so often, I repeat not at all,
But sum it up briefly, "My God and my All."

However, it seems only right and quite fit,
To say something more than this wee little bit,
Bright Light is the meaning of dear Clare's name;
It prophesied well of her future great fame.
At eighteen, she left wealth and family and fled.
At the Portiuncula, she donned a coarse habit instead.
Shorn of her tresses, she then made her vow,
And said to her family, I cannot leave now.

Her dear Sister Agnes soon after came too,
And oh, how the trouble at home did then brew.
But the passionate outburst of rage soon did cease,
And followed contentment, sweet love and deep peace.
Years passed, Favarone, her father was dead.
Hortulana, her mother, the Poverty wed.
And young sister Beatrice, with long cherished desire,
Soon joined her clear voice to the glad chant in Choir.

Did you ever hear of such a strange prodigy,
As a mother and three daughters of the same monastery?
Lady Clare was the Abbess, and right sweetly did rule,
(Though her personal austerities might seem somewhat cruel).

It was all for the love of Christ Jesus, Our Lord,
And in this all Poor Clares are in perfect accord.
The gates of God's mercy never are closed,
But we must pray and be humble, far more than supposed.

St. Clare worked such wonders, real miracles, too.
Her blessing cured lepers and sick not a few.
A nun in her convent had headaches severe,
A prayer of the Abbess brought peace and good cheer.
And wonder of wonders - the like never was heard,
A cross on the bread at the sound of her word.
The blessing she gave at the Pope's own request;
Her faith and great sanctity were proved with the test.

Infirm as she was for twenty-eight years,
She labored and prayed in this valley of tears.
About twelve hundred and forty, the Saracen hoard,
Brought death and destruction with arrow and sword.
With Assisi in danger, and San Damiano no less,
All turned to St. Clare for sure help in distress.
Though feeble in body, her spirit was strong;
And a prayer from her heart opened Heaven ere long.
The sweet Voice of Christ in the Blessed Sacrament said:
"I will always protect thee." How the Saracens fled!

At last came the hour of greatest delight,
When upward to heaven she took her fair flight.

The Queen of all virgins most tenderly spread,
A mantle of beauty all over her bed.
Clare's face was transfigured, her transport most sweet,
When the time came forever her Bridegroom to meet.
Seraphic her love at the final great Call,
When she breathed out for always: My God and my All.

Sister Louise Belecky, O.S.C.
Duncan, B.C., Canada
(around 1960)

A Journey Up The Mountain

My vocation story is best captured as a person who fell out of a hearse and kept on walking. As a child and teenager I battled the illness of rheumatic fever. At the age of 12 the doctor told my mother and dad to plan my funeral. I obviously survived! The doctor's next good news was my life span would be 45 (if I were lucky). I am now 75!

I entered the monastery at age 20 with a "phony" health certificate, so strongly did I feel drawn. Looking back at those early years I think what I really had and still have is "romantic" fever. I came from a large, Irish, loving Catholic family where religion was highly developed. I saw my parents affectionate with each other and I had no doubt that my Irish dad idolized my German mother. It was easy for me to imagine how God felt about me. I was very loved and cared for, especially as an invalid. I remember especially how my sensitive Dad promised me a new dress when I got out of one of my many hospital stays. My mother and dad were daily communicants at the early Mass at our parish church about half a block from home. As a family, religious devotions of prayer and ember days and all the traditional practices of a Catholic upbringing touched me on a daily basis. My illness took me from the normal lived experience of a large family since I could not join in the games and fun of my siblings. Instead of interacting socially, my comfort came with playing alone, reading books, and developing my artistic talents. Solitude at this early age led me to experience a joyful interiority: God was my playmate and my confidante. With nine siblings running and playing I am sure I also craved a little peace and quiet!

As I reflect now, after nearly 60 years of living the Poor Clare life, I know that God has given me the courage and strength to keep on walking with the various "touches" of death in my life. There have been changes and challenges and I continue to know God as more than a playmate - as a constant soulmate.

I am grateful to St. Francis and St. Clare and all the vibrant Franciscan men and women that have nourished me along the way, especially the women I live with today. As we journey up the mountain of love along with all the Franciscan family, I pray for our deepened communion in the spirit.

Sister Laurene M. Burns, O.S.C.
Saginaw, Michigan

"If you suffer with Him, you will reign with Him."　　　　*2LAg 21a*

My Red Dorsey Pumps

No thought, word or deed could give adequate expression of my gratefulness to God for the gift of my holy Vocation. God's grace can certainly give perfect shape and shading to our lives. What might have been a weed or wildflower can become a cultivated rose.

I lived a stone's throw from our monastery. Two months before I entered, if anyone said I was destined for this life, I would not have believed them! Once having entered, I would not change places with the President's daughter.

Living in the world, I was of the world with all its power, paint and false promises. I smoked for five years, but giving it up meant nothing to me. At my family visit, my brother used to blow smoke through the grate into my face...perhaps to tease or tempt me, but it did not bother me one way or the other.

Swimming and fancy diving were among my favorite enjoyments. If ever I had to give them up, I thought I would die—I've given them up and I am still very much alive! I danced about four nights a week and would rather dance than eat; now I think that is a waste of energy. I did a little horseback riding which I found very enjoyable; perhaps when I get to heaven St. Paul will let me ride his horse.

The magnet of glamor attracts many by its make-believe happiness. So many join the parade of great pretenders; the show is all on the outside. Pretending to be happy never produces happiness. Once I set my eyes on a pair of red Dorsey Pumps and could not wait until I got them on my feet. After I looked at them, I realized they did not make me one bit happier, which showed me the emptiness of temporal and material goods. When I took my physical examination for my entrance into the monastery, the doctor told me not to give my red shoes away. I suppose he had doubts about my perseverance. He knew about our life and its austerities.

I am very happy to say that I have now been in religious life for 58 years — and I would not trade one single day to be back in the world. These years have been the happiest and most fulfilling years of my life. God has been very generous with me and with His help and grace, I wish to continue to live a life that is pleasing to Him. I am grateful for His continued grace to help me live life with the desire of imitating the refinement and culture of Our Lady...her unselfishness and humility, her love and desire for the salvation of souls and their sanctification. God's grace can make a beautiful melody of our lives and our cooperation can make perfect harmony!

Sister Mary Constance Mangan, O.S.C.
Langhorne, Pennsylvania

"If you die with Him on the cross of tribulation, you shall possess heavenly mansions in the splendor of the saints."   2LAg 21c

A Dream Come True

When I was eight years old I started to go to St. Agnes' Catholic School. My teacher's name was Sister Lorenzo, O.S.F. from Oldenburg, Indiana. The first time we received our report cards we had to change places. I was in the second row and had to move to the first row. I saw that Sister was watching me. When I was all settled she stooped down and whispered, "be real good now. The Blessed Sacrament is right above you." This thought never left me, and I believe this was the beginning of my vocation.

One night I had a dream that my mother and I were going some place. I was ready to go and she wasn't so I started toward the front door. I looked out and there was a great crowd of people walking out in the street. I joined them and we walked and walked and then I noticed that I was all alone. I looked up and there was Jesus coming toward me with His hands and arms outstretched toward me and I reached my arms out toward Him. As I was about to touch Him, He disappeared. I stood there all alone and I thought to myself: If I had waited for mother, I wouldn't have seen Him. With that, I woke up.

I told our priest that I wanted to be a religious but that my mother was very much against my being a nun. He said: "if God wants you to be a religious, He'll take care of your mother."

My pastor told his assistant I was going to the monastery. He could not believe it. Financially we were well provided for but my mother was crippled; I was the only child. My father died when I was only nine.

I had never seen a Poor Clare. On the Feast of the Portiuncula, a neighbor lady asked me to go with her to the Monastery. The first Sister I met was Sister Mary Antonia. I told her I'd like to enter and she said, "You stay here a minute, I'll be back." In a very short time she was back and said, "Mother will see you now." I went in and there was Mother Mary Francis at the grate. She said, "If you are obedient, child, you'll get along." She wanted to take me in right away but I told her I needed to spend that winter with my mother. She had to have time to get someone to stay with her.

On May 12, the Feast of the Patronage of St. Joseph at that time, I entered as an extern sister, and they had to add a piece to the table. There were nine of us at that time.

One day as I was working in the yard, I was called in to see Reverend Mother. She asked me if I'd like to receive the holy habit. I said, "Oh, yes!" On November 21, 1943, I received the holy habit and was given the name of Sister Mary Rose of the Holy Family. I made my First Profession on March 19,1945, and my final Profession in 1948.

I have had a special devotion to our Blessed Mother all my life. When I was in the seventh or eighth grade, there was a statue of Mary on a landing of the stairs in my school and I always prayed, "Mother of God, remember me." Now I pray to her, "remember me and all mankind."

Sister Mary Rose Edmond, O.S.C.
Evansville, Indiana

"In the Book of Life, your name shall be called glorious among all."
2LAg 22

Sister Mary Rose Edmond went home to Jesus just prior to publication.

The Story of My Vocation

Ours was a very Catholic family. I can't remember a time when we didn't live within a block of the church and Catholic school, and as soon as I was "of age" I attended daily Mass with my mother. In addition to immediate family there were my maternal grandparents and several of my mother's brothers and sisters living within a three-block radius of us. I am still not sure whether some of the people who were common visitors at my grandparents' home were related to us or not. They were just part of the backdrop of my life with St. Gabriel Church at the center of it all.

The Sisters of Mercy were models for me at St. Gabriel School, but the seeds of my vocation came more from their numerous visits to our home. To see the sisters in a relaxed moment, staying longer to hear the end of the baseball game on the radio, or to chat or have a cup of tea, helped me realize that behind the yards of serge and the starched coifs and guimpes were real people, filled with joy.

Most of the girls in our neighborhood were either getting married or going to the convent right after high school. I followed suit by entering the Sisters of Mercy. Being a sister was something I always knew I wanted to do. I did like to go out with "boy friends" to movies, high school dances, or football games, but that was just for fun. In my serious moments, times late at night sitting in the big overstuffed chair in our parlor, I knew that I wanted to give my life to God totally as a nun.

In hindsight I realize that the novitiate at that time was a monastic experience. I loved it, even with some of the weird practices. When we were thrust into a classroom after about two years of various education courses, it was a rude shock. It took a few years for me to come to grips with the idea of discipline in the classroom, but then I began to love teaching and continued to love it for many years.

By the 1970s everything was changing in the Mercy community as well as in the Church after Vatican II. I was shaken to the core with questions not only about my vocation, but about faith itself. Around this time a sister whom I deeply respected told me she was organizing a summer house of prayer and asked if I were interested. Realizing that I needed time to sort everything out, I accepted. This was the beginning of a series of things: my first directed retreat, finding a spiritual director, a 30-day directed retreat a couple of years later, and an experience of a futurology in ministry program for six weeks with eight other Sisters of Mercy. Each of these had a deep impact on my life, but surprisingly, it was the last that impacted it most profoundly. I will describe it shortly.

In the summer of 1976, the summer of the American Centenary and the tall ships, I and eight other Sisters of Mercy were asked to go to Salve Regina College in Newport, Rhode Island for six weeks. We were to work with Warren Ziegler, who was to lead us in a Futures experience. The expectations were, I think, to get some kind of "handle" on the future of the community.

What happened for me was totally unexpected. As the summer progressed, I kept envisioning the future of the Sisters of Mercy with the others, but what I saw as my own future was in a totally opposite direction. My future I found lay in a more contemplative life, a life of deeper prayer with less external ministry; that of the Sisters of Mercy would be expressed in more and broader service to those in need, albeit service supported by prayer.

I had been going to the Cenacle Retreat House in Warrenville, Illinois, once a month for a weekend of prayer and direction. After several years I had a session with Sister Winifred who listened intently for a while and then said bluntly, "Maryalice, what you are looking for is a Contemplative community. Why don't you find one?" After the shock, denial, and confusion wore off, I had to admit that she was exactly on target. Thus began a new search.

Now forty-seven years old, I didn't think there was much hope of my being received into any contemplative community. I haphazardly wrote to a few people, Sr. Marie Beha in Greenville among them. I had read some of Marie's articles in various periodicals and began a correspondence with her. In time I wrote to Marie and asked her if I could come to Greenville for a visit. My friends were shocked, but then supportive. It was not an impossible dream. After a visit to Greenville, I was ready to begin the painful process of transferring to the Poor Clares in August 1978.

From the beginning I *knew* that I was *home at last*, both as a Poor Clare and in the Greenville community. Although the transition was not without cost, the joy and peace, the certainty that this was where I belonged overcame all else. It was a perfect fit. Soon after the canonically required three years, I received permission to make solemn vows as a Poor Clare.

You may think this is the end; however, my vocation story has yet another chapter. Twenty years later, in April of 1998, I was asked to be part of a fact-finding group. The bishop of the Great Falls-Billings diocese in Montana had invited our Federation to make a foundation in his diocese. Something inside of me was moved by the very real desire of the people for a contemplative group. The strong Native American presence and the wide-open spaces also impressed me more than I realized.

I couldn't let go of the experience. I felt called to be part of it myself when the Federation approved of it. During a time of retreat I had the opportunity to discern this with my spiritual director. Later, after sharing my desire with Sister Rucia, our abbess in Greenville, and the community, I received both affirmation and support. Finally, in September of 1999 four of us, sisters from four different monasteries along the east coast, set out in a rented car for our new home in Great Falls, Montana.

As I write this, our community looks forward to the completion of our monastery. It is my dream and fervent prayer that this monastery will continue to provide the prayer presence of Poor Clares in Montana for many years to come. I am grateful to be a part of this exciting new foundation. It is but another part of the history of my vocation to give whatever God asks of me. An excerpt from Isaiah summarizes God's call to me. There is no end to the surprises God has in store for each one if we are willing to say "yes" continually:

"Do not remember the former things, or consider the things of old. I am about to do a new thing; now it springs forth, do you not perceive it?" (Isaiah 43:18, 19).

Sister Maryalice Pierce, O.S.C.
Great Falls, Billings, Montana

"My dear children, I guarantee you will not suffer any harm. Just have confidence in Christ." LegCl 22f

My Vocation

I come from a family of ten children, five girls and five boys. The boys all got married and the girls all went to the convent. Dad said: "Let them all go." He knew we were a religious family.

When I was in grade school, Sister asked some of the girls if they wanted to be a religious. We had a Benedictine Sister from Ferdinand teaching at school. I loved her and wanted to be a sister like her one day.

I had three sisters from my own family who were teaching at Ferdinand and I was very proud of them. In the summer we would go to see them. After going several times I knew that wasn't the place for me.

God spoke to me through creation and led me to the Monastery of St. Clare. My parents gave me their permission to enter. My mother took it hard. I was happy that there were so many young Sisters in the Novitiate. I loved it right away and knew that was where God wanted me and I'd be happy there.

Our work here is making altar breads, and I enjoy this work. We have Exposition of the Blessed Sacrament on Sundays and first Fridays. We do have free time for sewing, praying in the Chapel or other work. I have a little garden where I can be by myself and enjoy some fresh air and sunshine.

Sister Mary Elizabeth, O.S.C.
Evansville, Indiana

"Very frequently while she was prostrate on her face in prayer, she flooded the ground with tears and caressed it with kisses so that she might always seem to have her Jesus in her hands on whose feet her tears flowed and her kisses were impressed." LegCl 19:94

God Calls

The call of the Holy Spirit and of divine grace is very hard to put into words when the heart itself can hardly understand it.

I was in high school, and a public high school at that, when God's mysterious call began to work in my soul. My high school years were spent when World War II was raging and the country was engaged in horrific struggles on two continents. Almost no family was untouched and people turned to God for solace and guidance. God was the only one who had any answers to the chaos. All my cousins were in the armed forces and loneliness was felt by all. My own family was going through heavy trials, especially my mother who had to go to work. I had to take care of my younger brother and do the housework.

I think I really got my vocation from my mother, who was deeply religious and fervently devoted to the Blessed Mother. What impressed me in those days was "what does it profit a man if he gain the whole world and suffers the loss of his own soul" (Matthew 16:26). I thought of so much suffering and how it could all have been avoided if people lived a truly Christian life. The passion of Christ and the Rosary constantly occupied my mind. This led me to a contemplative vocation.

I became deeply impressed with the life and ideals of St. Francis with his total love and abandonment and self-emptying. I enrolled in the Third Order of St. Francis at St. Francis Church on 31st Street. I was in love with the spirituality I saw at St. Francis and in all the friars I met, among them missionaries to Brazil and a friar who had been expelled from China by the communists. At this time my spiritual director, who was not a Franciscan, steered me toward the Poor Clares in the Bronx, New York. How fortunate I was in having such a deeply spiritual director.

After high school I entered the monastery and had the great privilege of living with the founders of the New York community, Mother Mary Seraphim, Sister Mary Pius and the pioneer members. Mother Mary Teresa was my novice directress, and she began the foundation in Annapolis, Brazil, in 1963. These sisters were of the "old school" and possessed a deep spirit of prayer and sacrifice, love of God and zeal for the salvation of souls. No sacrifice was too great as it brought about the reign of Christ and the salvation of souls.

It was marvelous to see how Divine Providence nurtured the community and caused it to grow and expand to the day in 1963 when we sent our first sisters to Brazil. Later came foundations in Stamford, Connecticut, Cincinnati, Ohio, and Great Falls, Montana. Some time later the sisters in Brazil returned to New York indicating that God had other plans for our community. His ways are mysterious, and God often writes straight with crooked lines.

We are called to deepen our interior life and trust in God to cope with the chaotic events of our lives today. The loss of our monastery in the Bronx caused me great pain. A devastating fire that destroyed all furnishings and treasures in storage in August 2002 was another crushing blow but also a great grace.

Now we are poorer than ever and just living on the providence of God from day to day. We are living more as St. Clare wanted. We really are "Poor Clares." I am now on fire with the desire to save souls and to save our beloved country.

As I say the *Oblation of Divine Love* of St. Therese, I am conscious of the fact that with the little I have, Jesus can do so much. I am struck with what Therese said in her *Oblation*: "I come before You with empty hands." "Jesus Himself will be my sanctification." "Behold me through the face of Jesus and in His heart aflame with love."

I can only abandon myself into the hearts of Jesus and Mary. Dom Marmion wrote, "The more one remits oneself into God's hands for everything, the more one lives in absolute dependence on His good pleasure, the more he supports and blesses us in all we do." "While you seek the kingdom of God in you for His glory, He will look after all the rest."

Confidence in God and consecration to Mary are my main support and goal in life as we press on to fulfill whatever God has in store for us.

Sister Mary Philippa of Jesus, O.S.C.
New Rochelle, New York

"...my most beloved sisters, do not wish to have anything else forever under heaven for the name of our Lord Jesus Christ and His most holy mother."
RCl 8:6

A Family Affair

As I recall my entrance day (fifty-four years ago), it was not a dramatic experience! The transition from layperson to religious went very smoothly. I was twenty-five.

My late father's sister, Eileen, had become a Poor Clare postulant immediately after high school graduation day. A close cousin soon followed Eileen's example; eventually Genevieve became Sister Saint Clare. My own sister became Sister Mary Agnes (after the sister of our holy Mother Clare). Her cheery letters home probably were a factor in my decision to come to Massachusetts and, following a brief stay at an uncle's home, join the Order. I chose to try the life of an Extern Sister.

Sister Mary Immaculate, an Irish immigrant, had preceded me as an Extern Sister in the Lowell community. Together we helped the community by sewing (using a sewing machine and doing hand sewing occasionally).

After a while we Extern Sisters would help out by taking care of some shopping details. Occasionally we would attend a Mass for a deceased benefactor of our community.

I have never regretted having joined the order. I am always grateful that my older sister, an aunt and a cousin led the way...for following Francis and Clare as religious.

Sister Mary Anthony Burke, O.S.C.
Andover, Massachusetts

"Jesus told me He would always defend us." *LegCl 22b*

Be A Poor Clare

My parents desired that I should find my vocation in life and my mother especially prayed for that. Our junior year in high school, Sister Bruno, O.P., told her students to pray for vocations to the priesthood and religious life; she said that we did not have to pray for ourselves to have one but just to pray for vocations.

A very early memory is putting a cloth over my head looking in the mirror and telling my dad that I was going to be a sister. I had that desire and when my father began to work for the Poor Clares, he took me with him sometimes to milk the cow. We took the milk to a dark room in the basement of the monastery and that did not leave a good impression on me. I did not want to be cloistered!

As a freshman in high school our parish orchestra played for an event and afterward a movie on the *Little Flower of Jesus* was shown. One of the sisters said maybe I would be a nun. I said maybe! I remember praying to know my vocation after I had received the Sacrament of Reconciliation at the age of fifteen. I distinctly heard the words, "Be a Poor Clare." I told no one about this experience. I thought that I was too young to enter at that age. I thought that I should finish high school first.

I also had a great desire to have one year of college so I worked a year in order to have the money to do that. I spent a year at Duchesne College in Omaha which was a year of grace. I was taught by the Religious of the Sacred Heart who were devoted to the Sacred Heart of Jesus. There were too many students for the Sodality so the freshmen could join the "Children of Mary." We studied the life of Christ, Logic, a Humanities course that was inspiring, and instruction about the spiritual life. Our retreat was conducted by Fr. Rooney, S.J., who had a deep devotion to the Holy Spirit. He told us that if we were devoted to the Holy Spirit our lives would be changed. It was to be the grace that I needed to decide to apply to be a Poor Clare nun.

My grandmother was a member of the Third Order Franciscans and she died just before that retreat. She was in a coma the last few days before she died and when we would sprinkle her with holy water, she would make the Sign of the Cross. That made a strong impression on me too. My mother's aunt, Sister Henricka, was a religious of the Precious Blood of Jesus. She had encouraged my mother to become a religious. When the date chosen for my Solemn Profession as a Poor Clare nun was the Solemnity of the Most Precious Blood, July 1, 1953, I thought that she had something to do with it!

Sister Mary Clare Brown, O.S.C.
Omaha, Nebraska

"Just as the memory of her Christ was present to her in her sickness, so too Christ visited her in her sufferings."   *LegCl 29*

Reflecting on the Past — Living in the Present

Once upon a lifetime there was a little girl who was nine years old. One Sunday afternoon she went with her mother to the Poor Clare monastery in Philadelphia to visit her mother's cousin, Sister Mary Ignatius. If you're wondering if I am the little girl, wonder no longer. Since Sister had many nieces and nephews, there was only time for a quick hello. However the memory of that visit would last a lifetime. The rough habit and the cord pulled on my heartstrings. It was at that moment the seed of a vocation was planted in my tiny soul. Today religious writers would chalk it up as a spiritual experience.

Down through the years I stayed close to God and His Blessed Mother. On December 8, 1950, I entered the monastery in Philadelphia. My mother was heartbroken. She tried to follow me inside the enclosure door. It pierced my heart when Mother Aidan told her that she could not come with me. A few days later, the same two-edged sword pierced my heart. For the first time, I visited briefly with my dad in the parlor. As he looked at me behind the grate, tears came to his eyes. However, with the grace of God and the passing of time my parents were able to accept the separation. Everyone that came to our house knew that my parents had a daughter in the Poor Clares.

My reception of the holy habit, my profession and jubilees were special days in my life. Uppermost in my thoughts is the Sunday that my mother and brother-in-law drove me to Christ House in New York for a workshop. When the enclosure door opened and I walked out into the vestibule, my mother was waiting to hug me. For the first time in twenty-two years, I touched my mother's hair and kissed her. Yes, there was time out for tears. Another sister's relatives also were crying.

As I draw this sharing to a close, I believe that there is a vocation within a vocation. Everyone is called to a particular monastery. For me, it is here at our monastery in Langhorne.

Sister Mary Immaculate, O.S.C.
Langhorne, Pennsylvania

"...drive every noise away from the dwelling place of your mind so that you may cling to the depths of God alone."   *LegCl 36b*

The Greatest Gift

The greatest gift of my life, next to my faith, has been that of vocation. Many years ago, at the age of ten, I found myself bored and hot from the summer's heat and looking for something exciting to do. The only thing I could think of was not very exciting — visiting an older neighbor who lived alone!

I found her sitting on her front porch, smiling and look-ing into the distance. Being curious, I asked why she was smiling and her answer has been with me every day of my life. She said, "I just visited Sisters in Spokane who pray a lot and love God so much. They call themselves the 'Poor Clares,' but they are really the 'Rich Clares' because God is their life and they love Him so." Then she looked at me sit-ting on the step and said, "What do you think of that?" I didn't answer her question but said that I had to go home.

Mother was in the kitchen when I ran in the door. I went to her and announced, as only a 10-year-old can: "I'm going to be a Sister in Spokane." Nine years later I began a won-derful life, to which I can only say: *Deo Gratias* !

Sister Mary Rita Dolan, O.S.C.
Spokane, Washington

"Truly I can rejoice—and no one can rob me of that joy."   3LAg 5

The Little Book of Life

I went to church a lot and was asked by many persons to pray for them — which I did. After work I stopped by Holy Cross Church, my parish, and went up to the altar rail to pray for those who asked me to pray for them. One day my father happened to also go into Holy Cross Church, and he noticed that I was the only one in Church. At that time he said, "Yes, I was called to be a Nun".... I have been in the Monastery for almost 52 years, happy ones too; it has been a very grace-filled life, so meaningful and prayerful.

I never considered a religious vocation as my call. I am one of nine children, and I just took it for granted that I would also get married and have a large family. I am a twin and we were the middle children. I went to public school. However, our pastor started the Missionary Sisters of the Divine Child for the purpose of teaching us catechism. We were allowed to leave school on Monday afternoon for these classes when in grammar school and also in high school. I still keep in touch with the Sister who taught me, even after my being a Poor Clare for 52 years.

In discerning my vocation, I made a weekend retreat in Williamsville led by a Passionist priest. He suggested that we read a book during this retreat. I am not a fast reader so I chose the smallest book there. It was entitled *Princess*

Poverty, and it was about St. Clare. I did not know of St. Clare or St. Francis, but now I do, joyfully.

I also remember making a Novena to the Holy Spirit. I knew that I did not want to teach and felt called to a life of prayer and penance. I was given addresses of some religious communities. The first one I wrote to was in Philadelphia. I received a reply immediately with an application form enclosed. I completed it and celebrated with a delicious cup of coffee.

Somehow I felt drawn to the Franciscans. We did not have any Franciscans in Buffalo at that time so I had written some in other cities. The Franciscans are noted for their joy and love; this is how I wanted to spend my life while serving my loving Father, God, and my Lord, Jesus.

Not having traveled much, I did not know where Philadelphia was. It turned out that it took us 14 hours by car, which meant that those who drove me to Philadelphia had to stay at one of the Sister's homes, and they left for Buffalo on the third day of arrival. It worked out okay, thank God. I never saw the Monastery or met any of the Poor Clares, so this was definitely "blind faith." I was rewarded, though, and grateful for my choice.

My first sadness hit me shortly after I entered. A member of my family was undergoing surgery. We were cloistered and could not go home. I remember praying to the Lord and being able to get through this with a sense of peace. All did work out, thank God.

As for my joys...the privilege of my reception of the Holy Habit and receiving my new name: Sister Mary Francis of Christ Crucified; the first Profession of my Vows; my Silver Jubilee and Golden Jubilee were all truly awesome, exciting, prayerful, and delightful. The opportunity to see my family and friends at these times was so special and a first for many of them.

I have no regrets; just lots of gratitude and blessings to keep ever close to my heart with song and a dance. Amen. Alleluia!

Sister Mary Francis Tona, O.S.C.
Langhorne, Pennsylvania

"Virtue is brought to perfection in sickness."   *LegCl 39c*

From Fear To Love

I was born on April 5, 1934 and baptized Eileen Teresa Rowland. My parents, Jessie Dunlop and Peter J. Rowland, were born in Ireland. Because my father fought for the IRA and was being hunted when the Civil War broke out, he fled to the United States. My mother and oldest brother, Jim, followed two years later in 1925.

I grew up in Brooklyn, New York, with two brothers and two sisters. I fondly remember the times that I sang *Somewhere Over the Rainbow* in the backyards of our neighbors to get money to go to the movies on Saturdays. I was a bit of a free spirit growing up. I often took trolley rides and subway rides by myself. I never quite settled down in my studies until I realized I wanted to be a nun. I knew that meant I had to start studying. Therefore in the seventh grade I began to buckle down. I had a lot of time to make up. From the time I received my First Communion, I started going to Mass almost every day and decided I wanted to be a Sister of St. Joseph of Brentwood, New York. I entered the order in September 1952.

I was a Sister of St. Joseph for 15 years, during which time I was sent to Puerto Rico. It was a miracle I ever learned Spanish since I never studied formally. I seemed to have absorbed it and learned it more through osmosis. I was able to teach the fourth grade in Spanish. It was during these six years that my mother died, my father having died when I was a junior in high school. I had 15 grace-filled years with the wonderful Sisters of St. Joseph.

During my years in Puerto Rico I began to feel an inclination and then a strong inspiration to join a contemplative form of life. Although there were many obstacles (a certain reservation by my superiors, the sickness of my mother, etc.), the Lord in His providence cleared all the obstacles for me, and I was able to enter the Memphis, Tennessee Monastery of the Poor Clares on July 1, 1967.

I learned quickly that the life of a Poor Clare was one of faith and trust. I can remember vividly the Sunday morning at Exposition of the Blessed Sacrament in early February 1968 when I felt drawn to offer myself to the Lord in the words of St. Augustine, "Here. Cut here. Carve and burn me still, Lord, I'll do Your Holy Will." I felt strongly that God wanted me to be a Poor Clare but I was struggling with the adjustment to life in the Monastery. When I left the chapel that morning Sister Mary Paul, my Novice Directress, called me over and asked me to please keep the altar bread work going smoothly since Sister Mary Helen and Sister Mary Agnes would be going on retreat in preparation for their solemn vows the following Saturday. I felt very close to Sister Mary Paul since she also had transferred to the Poor Clares from an active order. She helped me very much and understood my struggles. However the day after the Solemn Professions were over, Sister Mary Paul became sick and died a month later. In my heart I felt a tremendous loss. Mother Annetta, the founding Abbess of the Memphis Monastery, died the next day. It was a time of sadness for the monastery.

At this time my prayer and relationship with Christ grew deeper and more real. Daily I was experiencing a great many graces in the midst of doubt, darkness and abandonment. Jesus was very close. His presence was felt almost physically. One day at prayer I opened to the bible story of the storm at sea. I felt this experience in my heart. The words of Jesus to his apostles became for me at that time a source of real comfort: "Do not be afraid." Another reading from Scripture that I opened to was from Luke 12. The providence of God and His care became so real to me and helped me pass through a very hard time.

In April of that same year I began reading a book on prayer by Father Everley. I came across a sentence that spoke to me. He said, "Did you ever say a prayer and God took you at your word?" Bingo! I immediately remembered the prayer of Saint Augustine: "Here. Cut here. Carve here. Burn me still, Lord, I'll do your Holy Will." This was a great lesson for me. The darkness cleared and the light came, and I felt peace in my heart.

Sister Mary Peter Rowland, O.S.C.
Huehuetenango, Guatemala

"Those who are weighed down by sickness and the others who are wearied because of them, all of you: bear it in peace." CantExh 5

The Story of My Vocation

As a child I grew up in a small village in western Pennsylvania. I did not have the opportunity to attend Catholic schools, but my parents saw to it that their children received religious instruction by sending us regularly to catechism classes at our parish church. We subscribed to several Catholic periodicals at home and I used to see ads of various religious congregations. From an early age I was interested in learning about the lives of the saints and other religious matters.

I would have loved to attend a Catholic college but this was not financially possible, so I enrolled in a state teacher's college. During my first year of college, when I was walking to Mass on Sunday with a friend, I confided in her that I thought I would like to be a nun. Jane gave me a holy card with a prayer for a vocation printed on it. Someone had given her the card, but she knew she did not want to be a nun. I kept the card in my prayer book and recited it now and then. As time went on I became quite involved in various activities at the college. Even though I led rather an intense social life, the thought of religious life never completely left my mind.

During my first year of teaching in a small town in Maryland, a friend took me with her to visit an orphanage operated by Catholic sisters. I experienced a tremendous sense of peace being with these sisters, a peace that lasted several weeks. I began to think seriously about becoming a religious, and I began to read books about the Catholic faith and religious life.

During my second year of teaching I lived with relatives in Trenton, one of whom was planning to enter the Poor Clare Monastery in Bordentown. It was through visiting this cousin at the monastery that I met the priest who was to become my spiritual director. Under his guidance I also entered the monastery. I have been a Poor Clare now for 50 years and am very grateful to God for my vocation and to all the people who had a part in directing me here.

Sister Agnes Valimont, O.S.C.
Columbus, New Jersey

"After I once came to know the grace of my Lord Jesus Christ through His servant Francis, no pain has been bothersome, no penance too severe, no weakness...has been hard."   *LegCl 44b*

That Your Joy May Be Full
(John 16:24)

The chatter of high school girls in the rear of the bus slipped into dreams for the future. I offered mine. I saw life as a wonderful gift we had been given, with only one chance at it, and all eternity depended on how we used it. I wanted to use this tremendous gift well and leave the world a better place for my having lived in it. They were all nods and yeas in agreement. This seemed like a good time to break the news that I planned to enter the Monastery of Saint Clare in Boston after graduation, convinced that I could do more for the world by prayer than by anything else. You'd think I was going to the moon by their awed reaction: "You're going to be one of those nuns?" I was 18 that day, but the idea of being a nun actually began a few years before.

Not one to procrastinate, I had headed for our small town library right after school one day to complete a book report so I'd be free for the weekend. I was exasperated to find only one of the required author's works left: Sarah Maynard's *Princess Poverty*, and I had no choice but to take it. Once I started reading it, I couldn't put it down. It was midnight when my mother came to investigate the light under the door. By that time I had almost finished my second reading, still absorbed in the love relationship between

Christ and Francis. There was this courageous woman named Clare who left everything to live Francis' gospel spirituality and attracted many others to do the same. I knew that day I wanted to join Clare, too, and follow Francis. But where would I find Poor Clares?

During the intervening years between the book and the bus, I dated and I thought about nursing, teaching and marriage. Everything looked good to me. Then I thought perhaps I could combine vocations by being a nursing or teaching sister, but dismissed the idea because it would limit the good I could do in a hospital ward or a classroom. I kept finding myself drawn back to that initial attraction to know Christ as Francis had and eventually realized I had to follow my heart and be a Poor Clare. At least I had to try. A life spent in prayerful union with God would make possible all my humanity longed for and all I hoped to do with my life. I searched a bit and found the Clares were right up in Boston.

We think we give up a lot when the Spirit draws us to a consecrated life and, at the time when we leave close family ties and all the good things we have loved, it really is a lot. We are made truly human to the extent that we give ourselves to others, and for the sake of others. In the same way, the totality of a Poor Clare's gift of herself to the love of God is the only explanation for the real and lasting joy she comes to know. It's only with the passing of the years that we come to realize that through this emptying process our hearts were being prepared for a fuller outpouring of the Spirit.

Francis was a good teacher of the ways of the Spirit, so centered in Christ, so completely given to God that he overflowed with joyful love. Clare reflected His teaching well:

"After I once came to know the grace of my Lord Jesus Christ, through his servant Francis, no pain has been bothersome, no penance too severe, no weakness has been hard." (Leg 44) I would learn this, too.

Fifty years have passed since I first embraced the simple, contemplative life of a Poor Clare, in the hope that I was doing something powerful with my life, something that would affect the world for good. I soon realized I was receiving far more than I could ever give on both spiritual and human levels. To be a Poor Clare calls for the total gift of yourself to God, your sisters and your world every day of your life. My girlish plans for the future never envisioned the flip side of a loving relationship with God and the giving of myself: an inner peace and joy that would far exceed my dreams on the bus that day.

Sister Mary Francis Hone, O.S.C.
Jamaica Plain, Massachusetts

"Listen little poor ones called by the Lord who have come together from many parts and provinces." CantExh 1

I Have Created You For My Glory

I was not a person who always wanted to be a nun. I would have thought that was a crazy idea for me. When I was quite young I felt a great compassion for the black people, both in their history as slaves and at the present time. I wanted to help them and make up at least a little for what they had suffered. After I graduated from high school, while I was working in a bank, I spent my Saturdays as a volunteer at Friendship House in Harlem. I'm getting ahead of myself.

I went to public school for the first eight years so I was used to being with black kids, Jewish and Japanese kids, etc. When I was 11, the war ended and the concentration camps were liberated. There was no TV at the time, but we went to the movies once or twice every week and there were always newsreels.

I was very struck by the pictures of the concentration camp and I wanted in some way to help those people, to be with them in their suffering and to do what I could so that those things wouldn't happen again. Being so young, I did not know how to accomplish this, but I didn't forget the suffering people.

A couple of months before my seventeenth birthday, I read a biography of St. Teresa of Avila. Two things impressed me most: I didn't know that one could have such a close relationship with God, and I hadn't realized my own responsibility to all other human beings.

I wanted to spend my life helping others, so everything quickly fell into place and I was convinced God wanted me to be a contemplative. Not only did **God** want it, I realized it would fulfill all my deepest longings, though I had never realized it before.

From the beginning of my vocation, I have always been very aware of the great needs in the world...the needs of individuals and of groups and nations. That's why I was in such a hurry to enter the Monastery and get started doing what I could to help. I know my efforts are not worth much but, united to Christ in the Incarnation, my life can be valuable. I think I'm living the life for which God created me.

Over the years, my ideas of being a contemplative have refined, strengthened and developed, but basically I still see my vocation as a close relationship with God and a chance to help others. I pray for everyone, but the ones who have influenced and inspired me most over the years are the Jewish, black and Japanese peoples.

I pray for people but I think that what is most important is that my **life** should pray. I don't think saying prayers or private prayer is enough. If I live the words of the "Our Father" then my life prays and it is the only way that I can be of use to God and everyone..."Forgive us our trespasses as we forgive those who trespass against us; Thy Kingdom come; Thy Will be done."

To live these words has meant some hard times along the way, but nothing ever happened to me that couldn't be used to give glory to God.

In the Creed we say that Jesus descended into hell, after he died to see the just ones who had died before Him. But I think that Jesus also descended into hell while He was on the cross. Scripture scholar Raymond Brown says that over the centuries people have tried to whitewash Jesus' words: "My God, My God, why have you forsaken me?" They said He always had the beatific vision and He couldn't despair, so we shouldn't take His words at face value.

But I agree with Raymond Brown that Jesus was actually expressing his terrible depression at that time, so we would know he had experienced everything horrible in human life. I've experienced the hell of severe depression, but why should I complain? After all I'm supposed to follow the Lamb wherever He goes and if a time in hell was good enough for Jesus, it should be good enough for me.

I want to mention something about forgiveness. When I was a child my mother didn't tell me the truth about my origins. All she really did was to make a big mistake. She treated me the way she would have wanted to be treated in those circumstances. We were very different and the secrecy and misinformation caused me great pain. She didn't do anything wicked; she just made a mistake. It took me 50 years to forgive her and to grow up. At the end of her life, we were fine.

I learned about forgiveness and now I don't think I could not forgive anyone and anything. I also think that life is too short to hold a grudge. When I went to the Social Security Office at 65, the lovely lady who interviewed me asked me, at the end, to give her a spiritual thought. I was not at all prepared, so I said the first think that came into my mind. I said that I think forgiveness is always important. She was pleased with that.

Long ago I read in a book by Caryll Houselander the words of the British wedding service: "With my body, I thee worship." I can say, especially when I have pain: "God, with my body, I worship you" but most important, I always say: "With my life, I worship you."

In 1974 I was very sick for five months. It was the closest I ever was to death. I was extremely suicidal and nothing helped, not medicine or shock treatments, psychotherapy, etc. Finally, the doctor found the right medicine and in two days I was sitting on top of the world. It usually takes weeks for the medicine to work. One of the sisters called it "spontaneous combustion."

At the end of that year, some of us were sitting around and saying what we had learned that year. I said I had learned that I couldn't be destroyed. Amen.

Sister Joyce Munson, O.S.C.
Greenville, South Carolina

"Live always in truth that you may die in obedience."   *CantExh 2*

Hearing The Call

My calling was a combination of a loving, praying grand-mother; a Franciscan Sister who awed us with stories of her work with Indians; a mother who went to daily Mass; and a dad who knelt down at his big chair to say his morning prayers with all of us moving about around him.

Further connections with Franciscans in high school strengthened my call, but it was the appearance of Thomas Merton's books that capped it all. After reading some of his works, I knew my call was to a cloistered community — but it must be Franciscan, and where do you find them?

My guardian angel was at work. Into my hands fell a small booklet listing Sisters and there in the middle was a listing for the **Poor Clare Nuns, Philadelphia, Pennsylvania**! I wrote to them and got an invitation to visit. I did so on a day when two sisters received the holy habit — such tim-ing! Things happened fast after that. It was hard being the first one to leave the happy family unit that was ours...but Mother was open to it, and so was Dad.

Entrance day was October 4th; the time was 3:00 p.m. and I went through the big enclosure doors to be welcomed by all my new Sisters. The years went by swiftly and my love for the Lord in this community of holy and happy Poor Clares grows daily!

In Clare's writings she calls her Sisters to be mindful of the whole Church, have a worldwide view, and this is true of us. We reach out to our sisters and brothers in every land and every place. What a joy it will be to meet all of them in heaven!

Sister Mary Alfred, O.S.C.
Langhorne, Pennsylvania

"Do not look at the life without for that of the Spirit is better." CantExh 3

My First Meeting With Franciscans

In November 1922, after a stormy voyage across the Atlantic, we finally reached New York harbor. My father, who had sailed from England a year earlier, and two of his sisters met us. After a few days of rest my mother took the seven of us to enroll us in school. There was a large public school just opposite our new home, but to my English mother that meant a Protestant school, and she was determined to enroll us in a parish school. It was almost the end of the first semester so we met with refusals from the first two Catholic schools. Nothing daunted, she asked an Irish traffic cop if he knew of any other Catholic school. We learned that the Capuchin Franciscans staffed the little German church and the School of Our Lady of the Angels just one block away.

We knew of Franciscans in England, but there were none where we lived. It was a moment of grace, for the Friars were to have great influence on our whole family through their kindness, solicitude and wonderful pastoral care. We were not treated as strangers by our schoolmates or neighbors but rather welcomed, and soon we felt quite at home.

I owe my vocation as a Poor Clare to the teaching and wonderful example of the Capuchin Friars. I will never forget their care for the parishioners and school children, their outreach to the poor, and this of any denomination. They reached out to everyone. I learned of their missionary zeal throughout the world when we joined the Holy Childhood Society. We used to save every penny we could, and when we reached a certain sum, we turned it in to Sister. Then we had the joy of naming some child, in far off China or South America where the Friars had Orphanages. In our Readers in school, we learned about Francis and Clare. I would read about them later in life as a Poor Clare.

The Friars lived a gospel life and strove to attract people to Christ and His church. Like Francis and Clare they knew that this vision could only be lived in and through Christ by the grace of the Holy Spirit. They met Christ in their beautiful Liturgy, in the Scriptures, in their personal prayer and in Christ they experienced the unity of humanity.

On my first full day as a Postulant at the evening meal, the Testament of our Holy Mother Clare was read aloud. It seemed as though Clare herself and Francis were welcoming me home. When I heard the words: "and the Lord gave us our blessed father Francis as a founder, planter and helper in the service of Christ" (Cl. Test. 59). I knew that I was where I wanted to be and the two friends of my childhood were indeed welcoming me. I was called as the Friars were to live an evangelical life. As Madge Karecki, SSJ-TOSF has so truly stated in an article on our Call to Contemplation: "It is a life that unfolds in two directions:

one interiorly through contemplation and exteriorly through mission. They are not opposing forces, but rather two foundation stones of our charism." (*TAU* March 2002). Our Apostolic mission is to pray and work for the soul of the world.

Sister Fidelis Hart, O.S.C.
New Orleans, Louisiana

"I beg you through great love to use with discretion the alms which the Lord gives you."   *CantExh 4*

The Evangelical Life of Saint Clare

The Movement Grows

The first Franciscan women were from the people and for the people. Their small dwelling at the Chapel of San Damiano was on the edge of Assisi, readily available to the townspeople. They needed the people because they were sisters. The name sister makes sense when there are other sisters and brothers. Sister is a way of being in relation. This was not a new idea about life. Jesus talked about being brothers and sisters and mothers to Him, and all of us children of the one Father who is in heaven. When writing of the Christian way, Paul takes up this same theme of familial relationships. Francis made it a core value of his life and teaching. For Francis everything and everyone was brother or sister. Clare reflects this in the way she related with those around her.

At one time Francis was working at the Church of San Damiano, repairing the stonework. Francis predicted that women would live there whose lives would give glory to God. This was six years before Clare and her sisters came to San Damiano. What did Francis mean by saying that women by their lives would give glory to God? In the Hebrew Scriptures glory (*cavod*) refers to the power, honor and radiance that belong to God. In the Christian Scriptures glory has come to mean the pouring out of God's self in love; God loving us so much that God gives us his only-begotten son. The glory of God is shown in the passionate love of Jesus: his humiliation, crucifixion and resurrection. These are the deeds of Jesus the Christ bringing humankind to salvation. Jesus, the firstborn among many brothers and sisters, effects the transformation of ordinary life through participation in His suffering, death and resurrection. The human condition is transformed in God's infinite love.

The early years for the community at San Damiano were very ordinary. The sisters tended God's house through their prayer and received God's people at the door. There was a wonderful reciprocity between Christ in the chapel and Christ at the door. What made the mutual exchange real was that the sisters were as needy for the daily gift of bread and the inspiration of their neighbors as the people were needy for the spiritual support and compassion of Clare and the sisters. The sisters experienced the pains and sufferings of human existence and could embrace compassionately the sufferings of their neighbors.

Clare, Francis and the early sisters and brothers lived a high, deep, broad and inclusive spirituality. At the universities of Paris and Oxford two of the great Franciscan teachers put the experience of the early friars and sisters into beautiful theological teaching. Bonaventure wrote about all of creation as a reflection of God. John Duns Scotus wrote about the "isness" of everything that exists and the "this-ness," the specificity of all that is. We all share in "isness," for not to abide in "isness" is not to come from the creative energy of God. And we all express a "thisness," or unique-ness, as does everything that is or was or ever will be. These are marvelous truths but they could never have been stated unless there were some poor brothers and sisters at the beginning of the Franciscan movement who lived this expe-rience everyday with enlightened heads and loving hearts.

The early sisters and brothers lived ordinary lives. They took what life offered: the pleasant, the difficult, pain and pleasure. What made their lives attractive to others was that they had a focus and there was meaning to what they were about. They could tell you why they lived as they did. Their clarity, generosity and enthusiasm were irresistible to the ordinary people of the 13th century. And so the movement grew....

From Glory to Glory

*Sisters who served Our Lord in an active order
and then transferred to the Poor Clares.*

Embracing My Beloved

Vocations are like seeds that need to be planted by God and then nurtured by us. Vocations given by God must be enabled to grow by our faithfulness to this call. Let me make a few comparisons between seeds and vocations. First, the ground must be prepared for the seed. I in turn must be open to the seed of God's graces dwelling in my heart. The seeds are laid into the ground while the desires of my heart are laid before the Lord. The earth must be watered daily for life to grow and it is my daily prayer that gives life to the soul. Weeds are uprooted that prevent growth and temptations must be overcome that hinder the growth of grace to take place. Sun is needed for the flowers to bloom while grace gives the light of grace for the blossoming of our vowed life.

For some, a call may come early in life due to varied circumstances while others may hear the call later, possibly after reading a story of another's call or by prayer or just being open to God and the movement of grace in their life. At times, meeting another religious may inspire imitation and dedication. The saints often have led others to follow them as in the case of St. Francis and St. Clare.

To embrace a religious vocation one needs to love deeply, surrender freely, be generous, to trust in the Lord and then to let go and let God lead them. Jesus was both human and divine. In His humanity He always did the will of His Father. In following a religious vocation one gives their humanity over to God. God has to be their all. St. Francis often prayed: "My God and My All." Our desires must be for our Beloved. One must also have a healthy self-love in order to value what comes from within so that one can then reach out to those in need.

A vocation isn't being selfish. It isn't just to save one's own soul. We are called to praise God, to pray especially for the church, for our world and to reach out to the needs of our brothers and sisters either in prayer as a contemplative or in prayer and an active way as an apostolic religious.

My personal journey takes in all of the above. I was a rather pious child and a tomboy at that. I had two aunts who were religious and an uncle who was a Maryknoll missionary in China. They were to greatly influence my early years and helped to plant the seed of vocation in my life. I loved them and all three taught me much in my early years and certainly contributed to my spirituality and vocation. Beginning in third grade, I would get up for the early Mass and make visits to church at noon and after school as we lived almost next door. It was during one of these visits to Our Lady's altar that I heard my first call to give myself to the Lord in a religious vocation. I made a promise to say three Hail Marys daily so that I would be faithful to this "yes" to the Lord that I expressed on that day. Much surrendering and challenge beset this commitment in the years ahead. I just felt in my heart that I wanted to give myself to the Lord in this way. Yes, I knew what it was to love somebody and I had already given myself to the Lord, My Beloved!

In my high school there were many religious communities from which to choose but one community stood out for they seemed to be sisters of prayer. They were the Sisters of Saint Joseph from Chestnut Hill. After much consultation with my director-confessor and many prayers to the Spirit, I joined and became a teacher and then a practical nurse. These were good years, and I was happy in this Community and my apostolate. But in my heart I was yearning for what I perceived was the more in my surrender and love for Jesus. What was the Lord trying to say to me in my prayer and in my relationship with Him?

My first directed retreat was a conversion experience for me and I was drawn ever deeper into my spiritual life. I heard a call to give myself totally to the Lord in a cloistered contemplative community. Caring for my mother and aunt was to put that desire on hold for about fifteen years. My mother and aunt died just nine months apart. I was able to nurse both of them and was at their side when God called them to Himself.

About three years after they died I once again, while at prayer, heard a voice from within saying, "What is keeping you now?" My spiritual director told me to look into it as he knew how many times in the past I had discussed this desire with him. The discernment tore at my heart as I was happy with the community I had entered, with my apostolate, my friends and my life. The Lord knew what He was asking me to do and I was still young and healthy enough to attempt a transfer. To where was the question?

Never negate the power of publishing your community story in the Catholic newspaper. The Spirit was present to me. On reading an article concerning the Poor Clares who were moving to Langhorne from Girard Avenue, I immediately felt God was calling me there. I was so sure that I did not want to look anywhere else. Doors and windows began to open and what I felt was going to be impossible easily fell into place. God was in control of my life and I trusted totally in Him to lead me. Within the year, I entered the Poor Clares with the blessing of my community, family and friends. I am now a solemnly professed sister and am 50 years in religious life.

I am full of joy and happy to say that I have two loves now: two communities that have taught me the value of love, surrender and total giving of oneself. How blessed I am! My vocation is a precious gift from God and a pearl of great price that I treasure and will work at until I meet my Beloved and thank Him in person. All I had to do was to say "yes." Thank you, my Beloved, for teaching me to "let go and let God." "My God and my all!" St. Francis of Assisi.

Sister Joan Marie, O.S.C.
Langhorne, Pennsylvania

"…the holy joy with which she (Clare) was flooded within overflowed without because the love of the heart lightens the scourges of the body."   LegCl 18

Amazing Grace

"Amazing grace, how sweet the sound, that saved a wretch like me."

"Karen, I'm going back to the convent!"   "At your age? I didn't think they'd take women like us. Where is this place and what's it like?" "Whoa!   One at a time."

When I asked the abbess if I could enter the Monastery of St. Clare (at my age!), she said she had hoped for younger candidates but, if this is what God is sending, she wouldn't argue with Him.

My friend Martha Clare explained to me about her decision to enter a contemplative order after ten years on her own as an independent woman and after at least twenty-five years in an active order previous to that.

My life story was similar. I had been feeling the same call to return to my first love for some time, but I thought it was an exercise in futility.   Besides, I owned my own home in the city, had 10 acres in the country with a big house to rent, a fairly new car, an excellent job with superb benefits, near-by relatives and friends.   I was happy and having fun besides! Big city stuff, huh?

Was God calling me back? I'd find out! I wrote to the abbess and made arrangements for a visit. It was beyond my expectations even though it was like "camping out" in a new monastery that was being built around the nuns (not-so-new), 23 of them in fact. I fell in love. Was this for real? Everything started to speak to me: I became more certain.

Yes, even though I had been in an active order 27 years, had come back home to help my mom, suffering from a stroke until her death; and then, had built a whole new lifestyle with my career as a public health nurse, I knew this was it. Five more visits ensued before my date of entrance. I, too, was told, "We were hoping for younger candidates, but the community said they would be delighted to have you." What a welcome!

My formation period of postulancy, two-year novitiate, and temporary vows took place in Evansville, Indiana. Then God moved in yet another mysterious manner by guiding me to the Poor Clares in Victoria.

In Victoria, Texas, as everywhere among Poor Clares, the primary life of prayer and contemplation is accompanied by a practical daily way to support ourselves through a self-contained occupation within the monastery. Here also, Our Lord's spoken promise to St. Clare, to her sisters and to her hometown of Assisi is fulfilled: "I will always watch over you."

The occasion of my profession of Solemn Vows was for me a culmination of my desire for total consecration to God and to the Church which brings me, as a woman, to the highest form of commitment to the Trinity this side of heaven.

God wasn't finished with my journey just yet. In a few years, He brought me back "home" to my originating monastery in Evansville, where I now walk with my sisters toward the final goal of our consecrated life.

"'Twas grace that taught my heart to fear, and grace my fears relieved; How precious did that grace appear the hour I first believed!" ("Amazing Grace")

Sister Caroline Engbersen, O.S.C.
Evansville, Indiana

"Let women imitate Clare, the footprint of the Mother of God, a new leader of women." *LegCl Preface 24*

In God's Good Time

It was a wise second-grade teacher who sent a note to my mother saying, "Sunday is Mary's First Communion. Please provide a time and place for quiet and prayer for her on Saturday."

On Saturday, after breakfast my mother reiterated Sister's note, and we proceeded to the living room (used only on very special occasions) and my mother told me to pray and be quiet and think of receiving Jesus the next day.

Among the furnishings in the room was an immense framed picture of our Lady of the Chair. (This was the title for Our Lady seated like a queen, with the Child Jesus on her lap.) I believe this day of prayer began my vocation aspirations.

Thoughts of serving God took a back seat in the seventh grade when Sister told me she thought I should be a nun. Boys and a spirit of rebellion, typical of that age, caused me to try to divert my attention to other things.

In the eighth grade the attraction to serve God became strong again. The contemplative Passionist Nuns had a Monastery on the street that we passed frequently. This proposal to my mother and the pastor met with an emphatic: "No, too strict, I won't be able to see you," all in one breath. "Not while I'm alive" was my mother's final comment.

The Franciscan Sisters were my teachers in grade school. They invited gently. It was exciting to be part of the Preparatory Class for the Sisters of St. Francis of Millvale, Pennsylvania.

My life's vocation began to take shape during high school and postulancy. The novitiate, profession and preparing for the ministry of teaching followed one after the other. Intensive studies about Francis and his special charism, along with the example of the devoted Sisters, strengthened my resolve to make final profession.

Soon after, the rush of ministry took over. Prayer time before going to school and after a tiring day took its toll. True I came to serve God, but I hardly had time to get to know the Lord who called, drew, strengthened and loved me.

The crosses of a fatal illness of my father and my brother missing in action in the South Pacific drew me to the Lord more often and with an intensity never before experienced. My father died, my brother's body was never found and within six months, my mother met her Lord.

The contemplative life again presented itself. The antechapel at the Motherhouse was renovated and an immense mural of St. Clare was painted on the wall. Each time I saw St. Clare, surrounded by the friars, she seemed to beckon me to move forward. My spiritual director, my superior and the blessing of my parents (now deceased) as well as the Poor Clare Sisters of the New Orleans Monastery, all agreed that the Lord was asking me to be more enthusiastic and loving in my service to Him in the contemplative life.

I entered the Poor Clares on the Feast of the Sacred Heart 1954, the Marian Year. God has been generous with His gifts as well as the crosses. Following the example of our saintly older Sisters, I pray for the grace of perseverance to the end.

Sister Mary Blosl, O.S.C.
New Orleans, Louisiana

"May you always be eager to observe what you have promised the Lord."
BCl 15

A Reluctant Prophet

We have heard of the reluctance that several of the prophets (namely Moses, Amos, Jeremiah, etc.) felt when the Lord called them. I understand their response because I felt the same way when I first felt the call in my heart.

When I was a child I remember arranging a towel on my head to see how I would look as a Sister. Other than that, I had no thought of a religious vocation. I attended public school and did not come into contact with Sisters except in my weekly catechism class. After graduating from high school, I moved on to a Teacher's College where I specialized in public school music, a logical decision since I had taken piano lessons for many years. When I completed the course I spent seven years teaching music in various schools. It was during this period that the idea of a religious vocation came to me.

During the solemn Novena to the Blessed Mother we were encouraged to attend daily Mass and I believe that this practice, which I kept up after the novena, strongly reinforced my budding call to religious life. However, I was in an interior conflict because I had always conceived of my future as a married woman with a family and I fought the call for many years. Finally I remember saying, "yes" in my heart and from that point on, I felt at peace.

I had become acquainted with one of the members of the Sisters of St. Francis of Allegheny, New York. I felt attracted to the community so I requested admission in 1945. I remained in the community for sixteen years, teaching most of the time in a girls' academy. I liked the community very much and was happy with them, but I began to feel a desire for more prayer. Again, a long process of discernment ensued.

In 1961 I entered the Poor Clares of Bordentown, New Jersey, where I have happily remained.

Sister Natalie Hayes, O.S.C.
Columbus, New Jersey

"Bear the burdens of poverty patiently."   *Not*

A Long Road To The Monastery

I can trace my "yes" to Jesus' invitation to follow Him on my Holy Communion Day; I was 6 years old. Though the "yes" was said, the road that led to the actual commitment as a Poor Clare was not a straight one.

At the age of 18, I entered an Apostolic Group that brought me to Africa where the call to a life of prayer became strong.

For 18 years I journeyed with the Grey Nuns, Sisters of Charity of the General Hospital of Montreal. The spirituality was very Franciscan and my novice directress was a former Poor Clare. Though I knew from my Novitiate days that I was not in the right religious family, I kept on the journey as I was told apostolic groups needed Contemplatives in their midst.

While in Africa it became very clear that I could do much more for the people I was serving by prayer than by my actual work in forming nurses. This conviction became so acute that I knew I had to pursue the inner call. I asked to return to Canada and make a discernment process. Was it really God's will for me? An Oblate of Mary Immaculate priest agreed to journey with me through the discernment process. It was clear to him, right from the start that the

Lord was calling me to a contemplative way of life. Though not clear to me, the clarity came with time.

The day I transferred to the Monastery, I felt that at last I was home.

Why have I chosen the Poor Clare Way of Life? I have known the Poor Clares since I was two and a half years old as I grew up by the Monastery in Valleyfield, Quebec, and my family was close friends to the sisters.

Africa brought me back home to the Franciscan family not in my own French culture but in an English milieu on the West Coast of Canada. God's ways are not ours but so much better.

> Sister Marie Céline Campeau of the Cross, O.S.C.
> Mission, B.C., Canada

"May the Lord always be with you and may you always be with Him."
BCl 16

The Question and the Answer

When anyone asks how and when my vocation came about, I usually reply that it all really started in my twenties, while working at my job in a hospital with a Religious Sister. One day while on a break, Sister asked me **The Question**: "Did you ever think of becoming a Sister?"

But that answer is only a half-truth. God was preparing me my whole life in the ordinary and numerous events and through the good people He put in my path to nudge me on my journey toward the religious life.

About half of my elementary school years were spent in Catholic schools taught by Religious Sisters. Always I was attracted to and admired them; it never dawned on me that I might join them in the future.

At home, my grandmother lived with us. She went to Mass every morning, no matter the weather. I looked up to her as she made this daily sacrifice. At the time I made no attempt to imitate her.

During my days at public high school, so many good teachers influenced me for the better. They taught me to be conscientious and tolerant and to use my God-given talents for others. I could go on and on...!

To make a long story short, I joined the active Sisters that I had known at the hospital. It was a beautiful and rewarding life, yet I was drawn to the contemplative life. And so, I visited this Andover Poor Clare Monastery and knew at once that I had come home...come home to my earthly and to my heavenly home.

After fifty years in religious life, I am most grateful to God and to all those who helped me answer "yes" to **The Question**. This life of following St. Francis and St. Clare is a life of pure simplicity that needs to be experienced to be appreciated fully.

Don't be afraid to ask **The Question**, and don't be afraid to answer it.

Sister Clare Cordeau, O.S.C.
Andover, Massachusetts

"Bear the weight of humility humbly."   *Not*

Surprised by God

God catches me off guard; that seems to be the pattern of my vocation story.

It all began on a wintry March day when "Sister" was giving one of her periodic vocation pitches to our high school religion classes. Bored, I was using the time to pluck the fuzz off my green sweater. Suddenly I heard! This was my call! This was addressed to me. My life had taken a new direction. How should I respond?

That was the question of the next months. I began to pray, not the formal pious stuff of previous years, but a kind of eager searching, a need for time and space to be in relationship with this God who was calling. Eventually I talked to a priest and began to make plans to enter the convent of the Sisters who were my teachers.

Postulancy was a blur of adjustment. I was homesick and yet at home as I realized how the Spirit had been preparing me in the months before I entered. Novitiate was difficult, but I never seriously considered leaving; that initial call had been too clear. When profession day finally came I gave myself with all my heart. I still have the paper on which I expressed my desire for a life of prayer, poverty and community.

After completing my professional preparation, I began to teach high school and loved it. Days were filled with kids and classes and extracurricular activities. During the summers, I began work on a Master's degree and found myself at another chapter in my vocation story.

For the first time in my religious life, the structures were no longer there. I was on my own. Dutifully I continued to say the Office and get in the prescribed round of vocal prayer, hurrying through to get back to the studying I needed and wanted to do. One day in a moment of grace, I realized what was happening. I wasn't praying, never mind the words I was racing through. What did I really want to do?

Pray, I really wanted to pray. I started over again slowly and more deliberately. Next day, I had to make the same choice and so for the rest of the summer and into the next school year. Almost imperceptibly, my life began to change. Something was moving deep within and I sought spiritual direction.

It was also a time of professional transition for me as I moved from high school to college teaching. Again I loved it. These were also the years after Vatican II and I found myself in the thick of renewal work, excited about changes, committed to community, enjoying my ministry. Yet there was also something moving deep inside; I wanted "more" but I didn't know "more of what."

Eventually, I spoke to my major superior and she agreed that I move on to another apostolate. I accepted a contract with the Religious Formation Conference in Washington, D.C. Serving the needs of religious Sisters across the country meant travel, giving and planning workshops, being available for consultation. One of my first invitations came to present a workshop for the Poor Clares in Greenville, South Carolina. I was impressed with the community and enjoyed my stay. When they invited me to return the following year, I happily accepted little guessing the surprise God had in store for me.

The day I flew down from Washington was one of those "bad travel days" that can happen to anyone. A 7 a.m. flight meant a 4 a.m. rising; on the plane I found myself seated next to a woman who talked all the way, dashing my hopes for a quick nap. When I finally arrived in Greenville, the new candidate whom the Sisters had dispatched to meet me lost her way and we spent so much time wandering back roads. We missed dinner completely. As you may imagine I was not in a particularly pious mood when I finally got to the monastery and was invited to join the sisters for Office.

Yet as I knelt in that cramped choir stall, I was suddenly overwhelmed. I had come home! This was where I belonged; this was the "more" my heart had been seeking. I was so happy, so excited I could barely corral my attention enough to give the workshop for which I had come.

Somehow I managed and at its end told the abbess about my experience and my desire to live a life of deeper prayer, poverty and community. The attraction that had been there from first profession would find its completion in Poor Clare life.

Transferring from an apostolic congregation to a contemplative one was very difficult but so worth it. Novitiate helped me to adjust to a monastic lifestyle. Solemn profession transferred my profession and membership to this Poor Clare community.

These many years later, my vocation continues to unfold in all the surprising newness of each day. I am still challenged and excited by the call to give myself in a prayer-centered life for all God's people. The days are full and rich, hours of prayer and work alternate; silence and solitude bear fruit of love in community. I am grateful; my heart has found its home.

Sister Marie Beha, O.S.C.
Greenville, South Carolina

" Poverty in all things was in harmony with poverty in spirit which is true humility."   *LegCl 13*

Blessed and Highly Favored, Twice

The title of my story was chosen because recently when I went grocery shopping a black lady said to me, "Good morning, Sister." "Good morning to you and how are you?" was my response to her. She replied, "I am fine, blessed and highly favored." Those words she said have stayed with me. I often use them to meditate on and ponder on, how blessed and favored I have been to have a Poor Clare vocation.

We are products of our family of origin and our environment. My family was very religious and our home was decorated with religious art, some good and some bad. We never missed Sunday Mass, said the rosary at home during Lent and went to novenas and the Stations of the Cross and whatever else our parish was having. We boasted of our four religious sisters and one priest on my mother's side and one religious sister and one priest on my father's side. My family set a good example for me and helped me to make good choices in life.

I went to the Catholic parish school for twelve years staffed by the Sisters of Charity of Cincinnati. I loved the sisters and wanted to be a sister from the first grade. By the time I entered high school there were other distractions, and I lost the desire for a time. However, as graduation came closer, I decided to make a rosary novena of thirty days in petition and thirty days in thanksgiving to seek guidance for my future. I remember reading a book on the lives of the saints for girls and the two saints that I was drawn to were St. Therese, known as the Little Flower, and Saint Clare. Saint Clare stuck in my mind because of her love for the Eucharist. As a young child I had been drawn to the Blessed Sacrament and so felt Saint Clare would be a mentor for me. Thus I thought about cloistered life but was discouraged by my dad because of my mother's sickness.

My sister, Pat, had entered the Sisters of Charity of Cincinnati and was very happy. Because of her I followed in her footsteps.

After my first profession and my first teaching assignment my mother died. I spoke to my Superior and told her of my longing to be a contemplative nun. I explained to her that, although I loved teaching, I was trying so hard to really live a prayer life and be a good teacher. I felt like a rubber band being stretched in opposite directions. She did not encourage me to leave and enter a contemplative community but rather to stay where I was and do God's will there.

The desire kept coming back and in 1963 I wrote to a Trappist friend and told him about my desire. Again I was encouraged to stay where I was and do God's will where I was.

The years passed and I still longed for more not knowing what this "more" was. Then I was sent to Denver to be an assistant director of a day care center. Here I fell in love with the mountains and the beauty of Colorado. Looking at those mountains made me realize once again how fragile everything is and how God alone is eternal. The desire for a contemplative life came back even stronger, and God started to move the ball into my court so that I could discern and take steps to follow a call within a call.

It happened this way. The director, Sister Joan, told me one evening that she had decided to resign and go to Africa as a missionary, and she said to me, "Florence, I always wanted to do this and if I don't do it now, I never will." I was thirty-eight years old at the time, the great midlife crisis period and I thought, "Joan is right." I decided at that moment that I would become a Poor Clare for I thought, "If I do not do it now, how will I know if I do not ever try?" To my good fortune, I went, I tried, I stayed and I realize more each day how blessed and favored I have been, twice.

Sister Florence Vales, O.S.C.
Columbus, New Jersey

"Do not be afraid woman (Our Lord to Clare's mother, Ortulana)...for you will give birth in safety to a light which will give light more clearly than light itself."
LegCl 2:31

A Call to the Contemplative Life

Before and during my teenage years, I went to daily Mass very often on my way to Catholic school. My grandmother had a good influence on me as did my family, my school friends and my teachers. I remember talking to a Sister in the elementary grades about wanting to be a Sister. She asked, "Why do you want to be a Sister?" I answered: "I want to know God better." This desire stayed with me through my high school years but did not prevent me from going out on dates or going to parties. The desire seemed to dim when I failed my last year; I thought they would not accept me. Instead of repeating my year I was told by a priest to go and find a job. During the next two years I worked in an office. Wanting to finish my education I enrolled at night school. Due to illness in my family I had to stop night school as my evenings were taken with no time to study.

The second Christmas after I started working, the desire increased to give myself to the Lord in religious life. Breaking off with my boyfriend, I wrote to one of the Sisters who taught me in my second year in high school. I began to go to daily Mass more often and made visits to the Blessed Sacrament after work to pray. I talked to my parish priest about my desire. He advised me to see the Sisters who had taught me. After writing to them to ask to enter they sent me application papers. I also shared with the

Sister I knew and the Sister in charge of formation. I was accepted to enter the community in the fall.

After completing the year I missed in high school, I was sent to Teacher's College and received my teaching certificate. I also completed a BA degree during summer school courses and yearlong study. I became an elementary school teacher and taught in the schools where the sisters were in charge.

During the early years of my religious life, I made a 30-day silent directed Ignatian Retreat. This retreat was a turning point in my relationship with Jesus. I had been going to Catholic Charismatic meetings while at the university, and the scriptures began to come alive in me. They also came alive in my 30-day retreat. This experience opened me up to be more receptive to God's Word.

After four or five years of desiring to do God's will, He led me through prayer to want to live with a contemplative community for a few months or longer but not join. One of the sisters in our convent said, "I know where you would like to go." There is a Poor Clare community not far from the Benedictines in Mission. I knew of the Abbey in Mission but not the Poor Clares. So that idea stayed with me for several years. Then one morning when I was praying I felt that I said "yes" to God and would do whatever He asked me. I loved the sisters in my religious family and did not want to leave them. Finally at the end of the summer I decided to visit the Poor Clares. I talked to a sister and went to pray as they were having a holy hour and evening prayer. I could not get my nerve up to ask to live with them for a short period of time. After Christmas when I visited again, I asked to live with them for a short time, or extended time. I discovered that this was not done in this community. As time went on I felt that God might be calling me to join them. It was a very hard decision to make. Through prayer and reading the scriptures, sharing with sisters and priests, through retreats and days of recollection, I was given the strength to pursue my call to a contemplative community. I transferred to the Poor Clares in 1979.

Looking back over my life I can see the Lord was guiding me. Whenever there were difficulties I would look back and remember the times the Lord put His words in my heart: "Do not be afraid." (Matthew 28:10) "I am with you always until the end of time." (Matthew 28:20) "Come follow me, take up your cross and follow me in poverty" (cf Luke 9:23, cf Mark 10:21). "Come to me all you who labor and are heavily burdened and I will give you rest. Take my yoke upon you and learn from me for I am gentle and humble of heart and you will find rest for your soul." (Matthew 11:28-29)

Sister Ann Marie Moriarty, O.S.C.
Alexandria, Ontario, Canada

"Always be lovers of your souls and those of all your sisters."   BCl 14

The Treasure

The Kingdom of God is like a Treasure which
someone found hidden in a field.

I lived as a Sister of Saint Mary for 34 years, as a teacher for 20 years in the order and working in a parish for a number of years. I realized, however, that God was calling me to something more. For over 10 years I felt God's call to live a contemplative life. So I began searching for a Community of Contemplatives. I went to a House of Spirituality in Texas called Lebh Shomea (a Listening Heart) to discern a contemplative vocation. From there I went to Scotland to live with a hermit (Sister of St. Mary) for one and a half years. These experiences confirmed my contemplative vocation.

I became aware of the Poor Clares in Greenville, S.C., when attending a WRISC (Women Religious in South Carolina) meeting. I met a Poor Clare who invited me to the Monastery.

When I first went into the Monastery I was touched by the Sisters' life of prayer and their sisterly love. For me being received into the Poor Clares is a dream come to reality. Living in poverty, prayer and community with 16 other Poor Clare Sisters had brought me a deep inner peace and an inner joy. I have grown closer to God, myself and others.

St. Francis and St. Clare have become alive for me. Not being a Franciscan, I have immersed myself in learning more about these two beautiful saints.

I made my Solemn Profession in December 2003 and what a glorious day it was!

Sister Bernadette Marie Cappola, O.S.C.
Greenville, South Carolina

"Inwardly put on Christ."   *LegCl 4*

I Hear You Calling Me

When I was in the seventh grade a priest came to speak about vocations. I felt drawn by what he said and somehow I knew that God was calling me. I wish I could say the thought never left me, but that was not the case.

In high school I became caught up in all the activities around me: dances, dates, athletics, etc., to the point that, if it weren't for the grace of God, I might never have listened to His soft voice deep within.

I had just finished talking two of my friends out of entering the convent right after high school when I decided to take a walk by myself. In those days, even though it was in the evening, it was quite safe to do this. When I began to reflect on what was occupying my mind, I realized that I had been enumerating all the reasons why I didn't have a religious vocation. Then it dawned on me that I wouldn't be so caught up in this dialogue with myself about something that didn't exist.

At that moment I found that I was right across the street from St. Peter's Cathedral and since it was a Saturday evening I decided to go to confession. I had never gone to that particular church before. When I finished my confession the priest asked me if I had ever thought about entering the convent. After giving my excuses he simply said, "You should think about it."

By the time I got up to the altar rail to pray my penance I was in tears. Before I left the church that evening, I knew for certain that God was calling me to be a religious and then and there I accepted the invitation, never to deviate again.

On August 28, 1949 I entered the Franciscan Sisters of Glen Riddle, Pennsylvania. This was only the beginning of my journey because, even though I loved my vocation and the teaching profession, I felt deep in my heart that God was asking something other of me.

God's hand was so evident in all the circumstances that led to my entering the Poor Clare Sisters in Lowell, Massachusetts, that I never had the slightest doubt that this is where I was to give myself totally to God. I think I could write a book about all that preceded my entrance. There were many heartaches and joys and it was evident to me that God was directing everything! It was as though I was watching a great drama unfold, and all I had to do was consent to be there.

I must admit that there were a few times when I just wanted to walk away, but I knew that if I just continued to put my trust in my loving, merciful God, all would be well...and so it was...and is!

Sister Mary Malloy, O.S.C.
Andover, Massachusetts

"Everyone desired to serve Christ in a zealous fervor and wished to become a participant in this angelic life which so clearly shone through Clare."
LegCl 10:63

Eternal Spouse Of Jesus

When I was a small child in grade school, I thought of being a sister. After my graduation from high school, I had won a scholarship. A priest friend thought that I should accept that for the time being. My deceased parents left me $5,000, and with that, with money I earned working in a dime store, clothes shop, and teaching some small children piano lessons, I put myself through four years of college.

After that I wanted to follow my religious vocation but did not know just where to go as I loved prayer so much. My priest friend thought I could go to the Oldenburg, Indiana, sisters who had taught me in for 12 years. This I did and received the holy habit in July 1941. Soon after that I took a book off the library shelf about St. Francis, and in the back of the book there were a few pages telling about this Monastery here in Evansville. No one knows how that got there. As soon as I read that, I knew this was my true vocation.

I wrote a couple of letters to the Poor Clares and was accepted and received into their novitiate. My parents would have driven me here, but I wanted to run away like St. Clare. So I came here by bus. I thought I had told my parents about the grille in the parlor, but they did not seem to have remembered. A few weeks passed and my beloved adoptive parents came to visit me. When they came in and saw me behind the grate, my daddy fainted.

Although they were pained by my vocation here, they wanted me to be happy. When I planned to come, I gave away all my clothes and money, and mother said: "Dear, what if you come back?" I said "Mother, I am not coming back." I was so pleased with my decision that I never doubted that this is where my Spouse wished me to live with Him the rest of my life.

To show how our dear Lord gives back when we give Him: I had started taking piano lessons when I was about seven years old, and had been playing the organ since I was 12 years old. I thought I would never see a piano or organ again. How happy I was when I came here and the organ was in the cloister.

Here I have also helped my community by typing thousands of letters over a good many years. In my days they did not have any copier, so I typed them all one by one. I worked in the altar bread department and served as portress for a good many years and answered the phone and turn 24 hours a day, seven days a week. I was only too happy to have been able to do this ministry in helping people with their difficulties. By God's grace, some marriages were kept from divorce and some people returned to the church.

Now I am 84 years old and can no longer help in an active way but I spend five hours each day in the chapel.

Many years ago, Bishop Sheen paid a visit to our monastery. After the homily, he turned to our community and said: "What do you sisters wish me to talk about?" We all said, "Prayer." He was so pleased and he said: "Sisters, you do not realize how important your vocation is. Sometimes we priests go into a prison and perhaps a few men come to hear us, but you sisters can go behind the prison walls, bamboo curtain, iron curtain." We never forgot the dear bishop's words to us.

We pray for those who don't pray...can't pray...won't pray.

Sister Mary Anthony, O.S.C.
Evansville, Indiana

Be humbly devout and kind."   *Proc 3:3a*

Seven Shining Stars

I have served the Lord for more than sixty-five years in religious life. At eighteen I entered the Franciscan Sisters in Millvale, Pennsylvania and engaged in many ministries as a Franciscan Sister. I have fond memories of the many classes I taught and of my service to the Motherhouse in the role of sacristan. After twenty-five years as a Franciscan Sister I transferred to the Poor Clare way of life as lived in the Monastery of St. Clare in Memphis, Tennessee.

I composed the following "Praises" of my sisters in community. The Poor Clare way of life is built on two pillars - the mystery of poverty and the mystery of community lived as sisters. I offer these words as a hymn of praise for the wonder of living in community life.

These Seven Shining Stars Are Hidden in the Monastery of St. Clare in Memphis

Sister Mary Helen is the eighth wonder of the world. Whenever there is work to be done, she is the first one on deck. If there is a flood in the refectory, sacristy, or basement, she is in the midst of it with her sucking machine (wet vacuum). If the grass needs cutting she is sitting in the driver's seat, week after week keeping the grass under control. She heads the Ceramic department. As a cook, she has no equal. Even Betty Crocker must take a second place. She is an expert in canning. A variety of jellies, fruits and vegetables are canned early so that they will be ready for the Craft Fair in November in order to satisfy all the lovers of homemade goods. All disappears in no time.

You don't have to watch the TV, listen to radio or read the newspaper for the weather report or other major news when Sister Mary John is present. She is a walking newsperson. She can keep you up-to-date on any subject. She is also the sacristan. We do not have a regular chaplain. Sister must find a priest for each day of the month. Do we have communion services? Sometimes we do, but not through the fault of Sister Mary John. She does a marvelous job of finding priests in this age when the shortage of priests is a reality.

Sister Mary Anthony is Sister Mary Helen's assistant in the kitchen. She has already mastered the art of breadmaking which has earned for her a place among the best breadmakers in the world. She outshines all of us as a salesperson. She is a wonderful person to have in the gift shop and the most valuable. Sister Mary Anthony keeps things moving.

Sister Mary Alma drives a Cadillac (motorized scooter/wheelchair) and she goes whizzing by before the rest of us begin to move. Sister Alma shines as a seamstress *par excellence.* It is her claim to fame. Veils, habits, aprons and undergarments — all come from her hands perfectly made. She also sews dresses for dolls and provides them with a wardrobe to the great joy and sheer delight of the little children and the big children alike. These, too, are sold at the craft fair.

Do you believe that Sister Mary Marguerite is our local Beethoven? As she prepares to play the organ for Eucharistic Liturgy or the Liturgy of the Hours…listen…listen! Can you not hear the music of Beethoven? She can also work miracles. As the mail person, Sister Marguerite takes care of incoming and outgoing community mail. At Christmas time, we help her put 3500+ cards and calendars into envelopes and seal them. We work as a team in order to lighten Sister Marguerite's burden. Her Christmas work does not end here; it just begins. We are blessed by many generous benefactors, and a grateful thank-you note follows each donation.

Sister Mary Claudia is our Florence Nightingale. She is very conscientious about medications, the right medicine at the right time. She doles them out into individual containers neatly marked breakfast, lunch and supper. Nothing is too much for her when it comes to her patients. I admire her patience and her dedication to duty with tender loving care. Her laughter and smiling face makes taking medicine easier. What the nursing profession needs is more Florence

Nightingales like Sister Claudia. Sister Claudia is also secretary to Father David Knight. Many of you must know the famous Father David Knight from his many books. Through Father Knight and Sister Claudia these books find their way to almost every corner of the earth. Last but not least, Sister Claudia is also my secretary.

I, Sister Mary Regina, have the honor and the privilege of taking care of and cleaning the little chapel of Our Lady of Sorrows, which is situated in our monastery garden. There is a curtain behind the altar which is changed with the liturgical seasons. I make my daily pilgrimage to this Marian shrine in order to see if Mary wants or needs anything or if there is anything I can do for her. As in many of her apparitions, she is pleading with us to pray, pray, pray. Prayer can work miracles. Prayer can stop wars. Prayer can bring peace. Let it be our joy to lovingly respond to her requests. This little chapel, hidden behind the cloistered walls, is my pride and joy!

Sister Mary Regina, O.S.C.
Memphis, Tennessee

"For you will sell your fatigue at a very high price and each one of you will be crowned queen in heaven with the Virgin Mary."   CantExh 6

The Evangelical Life Of Saint Clare

"All of us, seeing the glory of the Lord, are being transformed from glory to glory..."
2 Corinthians 3:18

In the proceedings of Clare's canonization, Sister Amata, one of Clare's nieces who joined the community of San Damiano in 1228, recounts that Clare was assiduous in prayer and contemplation and that "When she returned from prayer, her face appeared clearer and more beautiful than the sun." Unlike Moses, who kept his face covered when returning from prayer on the mountain, Clare let the glory of God shine brightly on her face for the building up and encouragement of her sisters and brothers. Her prayer had a strong relational character. Clare's partner in prayer was Jesus. She was always looking at Jesus, whether prostrate before the Blessed Sacrament, weeping over the Passion of Christ, or identifying with Gospel stories about Jesus in her relations with others.

Over the altar in the little chapel at San Damiano, the image of Jesus was affixed to the cross bars of a 12th century icon. Jesus was depicted not in the agony of crucifixion but in an attitude of resurrection, ascending to the Father. "I ascend to my Father, and to your Father, to my God and your God." This was the crucifix before which

Francis received his mission to "repair my house for it is falling into ruin." Clare, also, would have prayed before this cross during the years of her long life at San Damiano. Communion with Jesus in glory, against the background of the cross, affected the whole person of Clare. In the Middle Ages the eyes were called "the queen of the senses." The image of Christ impregnated Clare's being through the doorway of her eyes. In this prayer of Christian contemplation, the body and the affections of her heart were most powerfully engaged and transformed. With a finely tuned heart Clare heard the proclamation and interpretation of the Scriptures. With this same heart, fully alive and passionately in love, Clare wrote to Agnes of Prague.

To read the four letters to Agnes is to feel the fire of her love for Christ. In the first letter Clare began with encouragement: "Be strengthened in the holy service which you have undertaken out of an ardent desire for the Poor Crucified who for the sake of us all took upon Himself the Passion of the Cross." In the second letter she specified her teaching:

"...gaze upon Him, consider Him, contemplate Him, as you desire to imitate Him. If you suffer with Him, you shall reign with Him, if you weep with Him, you shall rejoice with Him; if you die with Him on the cross of tribulation...your name shall be called glorious...."

In the third letter she wrote, "Transform your whole being into the image of the Godhead Itself through contemplation."

Before she died in 1253 in her final letter to Agnes, Clare focused again on the contemplation of Christ. Her passionate love for her "heavenly Spouse" overflowed in her passionate love for Agnes. Clare bade her friend goodbye "until we meet at the throne of the glory of the great God...."

He Who Chose Me
is Worthy of My Trust

Hopefully we all acknowledge this as true!

Gems

August 1953 — Desiring to embrace Poor Clare life in the Monastery in Omaha, I was unable to convince my parents I had a call from God. Turning to a Franciscan Priest and a Third Order Franciscan Sister, they wisely advised my parents: "If you don't let her go, she will always hold it against you. If you let her go and she finds she doesn't belong, she will be at peace. If she goes and belongs, you would not want to oppose God." With that I was free to enter!

September 1953 — My father and I were out doing work on our farm, providing water for cattle and feed for calves. I was simply enjoying daily chores and being with my father when suddenly his voice changed. "You have to promise me you will come home if you are not happy." I was surprised and startled at the burden of concern he carried. Somehow my heart knew where I belonged, and at that time I was oblivious of the cost to my family.

October 11, 1953 — Entrance Day. "What would I be like after five years in the monastery?" I wondered. I could not begin to imagine what 50 years of commitment would bring.

August 1958 — At last the day of final commitment came. In the Solemn Profession ritual, the words put on my lips and heart were: "In you, O God, I put my trust. Let me not be confounded in my expectation." Three times I sang this prayer and then gave myself to the Lord for life. I discovered over the years that continually I need to trust anew. It is an ongoing invitation from Our Lord. Day by day we are all called to put our trust in the Lord and we are not disappointed.

September 1968 — Vandals broke into the monastery which was then located in a ghetto area. No one was harmed, but the Sisters were unsettled by the experience. About two weeks later, a piece of artwork I had crafted crashed in the middle of the night. It was a textured work of stained-glass pieces mounted on a clear Plexiglass background. The motif expressed was, "From the pain of the dead wood of the cross came forth the vine of life." A wide red arrow intersected a brown cross. A brilliant green ivy flowed out of the cross. I'm not sure how others rated its artistic value, but it was the best work I had done. On that memorable night when the picture crashed down the stairs, the first assumption was that vandals had returned. The Sisters were relieved to find only a piece of art in shambles and kept saying, "Thank God, it's only Gabriel's picture." I understood the sentiment but couldn't share it. Gathering up the fragments I again put it back together over a period of time. Later it was given away and eventually went to Europe, or so I was told. I just hope it is firmly mounted wherever it might be.

Mid-1970s — Mother Teresa of Calcutta stayed with us overnight at the Omaha Monastery. She shared with us the heavy schedule she was keeping, and I observed how frail she seemed. As I was in charge of the kitchen, I asked Mother if she needed anything special for breakfast. Mother Teresa took my hands in hers, looked deeply into my eyes and said, "All I need is bread." The words went to my soul and it was a call to conversion. How much I needed to do very simple works, and all Mother Teresa needed was bread.

Jan. 29, 1986 — The day after the Challenger spacecraft exploded and riveted the nation's attention, I received a letter from Sister Antoinette Madden, O.S.C., from our monastery in Evansville. "Will you help me start a new foundation?" That letter had as much effect on me personally as the Challenger tragedy had the day before. It was the beginning of the unfolding of a new call from the Lord. In a year we would be established in Victoria, Texas. God calls in surprising ways. We have to be alert to hear His voice.

Feb. 2, 1987 — Christ is the Light of the World. This was the formal beginning of our Monastery in Victoria. We were well-received and loved by the people in this area. The warmth and love given us was amazing. We took root and began to love and serve our Lord Jesus and His people in a new place — "Let us build the City of God."

1989 — One day some poor children found our bakery; they came in and wanted a cinnamon roll. When they wanted more, I told them, practical-minded as I was, that we can't keep giving away cinnamon rolls. I told them to come back on Friday and we would share what we had not been able to sell. The next day they were back, saying, "We **always** get free cinnamon rolls here. I reminded the boys I had said to come on Friday. Their response, "We're hungry now." Being open to these children taught me much about material poverty, which I had never experienced personally. I still cherish our contacts with these children.

1991 — A priest of our Diocese asked me to remake a denim T-shaped multicolored lounge robe into a vestment. It reminded me of Joseph's many-colored coat in the Book of Genesis. This was quite a challenge! My original plan to find some matching shade of green material was to no avail. However, I did find some deep red material that blended well. When the sewing project was finished and Father tried it on, I held my breath until it was evident that he was pleased with the vestment. He remarked that everything has a way of becoming what it is destined to be. It's also true of us as our vocations unfold.

August 1994 — I was on a Franciscan Study Pilgrimage in Assisi, Italy. At La Verna we celebrated the Eucharist in a chapel built over the spot where St. Francis received the stigmata. The actual location was enclosed in diamond-shaped glass. I knelt near that holy place throughout the Mass. Here St. Francis had a profound mystical encounter with his Lord Jesus. In contrast my spirit was unmoved. It was a moment of learning *experientially* the interior life is truly grace working within, in God's time and place. We wait expectantly with open eyes, hearts and hands.

1995 — A memory of a retreat at our Spiritual Renewal Center remains vivid. A magnificent rainbow was arched perfectly over the chapel. "How fitting," I mused. I always loved nature and outdoor settings, so this beautiful bow in the sky was a delight. I began walking only to be surprised to notice the rainbow did not stay fixed over the chapel but seemed to move with me as I walked. The view encompassed by the rainbow changed, yet I was always at the center. Actually God is always at the center, and we are privileged to share life with Him.

2003 — Fifty years later, and I'm still on the journey. Priceless gems these days are, receiving the trusted confidences of those who come to us. Some are joyful, hope-filled, desiring good things for their lives. Others are sick, sorrowful, grieving or anxious. Perhaps all that is wanted is a listening ear and/or an encouraging word. These are lifted up to the Lord in reverence and trust and deepest of all, love....

Sister Gabriel Zwiener, O.S.C.
Victoria, Texas

"...I will never in any way wish to be absolved from the following of Christ."
LegCl 14g

The Lord's Way

I was born on June 13, 1970, in the department of Santa Rosa, Guatemala. I have two sisters and three brothers. My mother's name is Bernarda Valenzuela and my father's name is Dimas Morales. Both my parents are dead.

My vocation began to take form when I was seven years old. I was very sick and was cured by the prayers of a neighbor. I realized God answered that prayer prayed in a spirit of faith. Another experience I had when I was ten years old is perhaps clearer. At this time I visited a convent with a friend of mine. I had no idea what to expect. However, from the time I entered the convent I felt something very special that is difficult to explain. I knew that this was the life I wanted to live. My conviction was so real that when I went home I told my mother that I wanted to become a nun. The next day I asked my mother to take me to the convent. I made various attempts to enter, but I was always told I was too young. I remember the last convent I visited the superior promised to make an exception for me when I finished the sixth grade. When I graduated from sixth grade I returned to the convent but the superior was different and told me I had to be seventeen years old before I could enter. I was only thirteen at the time. I became very disillusioned and consequently forgot the whole thing. I finished my studies and lived a normal life of a teenager.

When I was seventeen I felt the call to be a religious once more. My father asked me if I still had the desire and I told him I did. He spoke to the pastor and the pastor took me to meet some Franciscan Religious. I became an aspirant for two years in a Franciscan Community, but I felt the active life was not for me.

A year later I moved to the capital, Guatemala City, to work. In the neighborhood where I lived, I joined a youth group conducted by a Franciscan Priest, Father Atilio Prandina. The following year a new friar came to the Parish and he took over the youth group. This friar awakened in me the desire for religious life once again. This friar helped me discern my vocation. He accompanied me to visit various contemplative communities. I did not feel attracted to any of them. One day Friar Francisco said, "Prepare yourself for a visit to a Monastery of Poor Clares that I'm sure you will feel attracted to." That was it. From the moment I entered the monastery I felt I belonged. I felt something special, a sense that I was where God wanted me.

I entered the Monastery of Poor Clares in Huehuetenango. I am the first Guatemalan vocation to persevere. I made my Solemn Profession June 13, 2001. I am sure that the Lord has guided me through this long process and has shown me the way. Each time I doubt or am overwhelmed by insecurity, the Lord in His infinite mercy reaffirms my vocation and makes me feel secure and realized in His great love for me. Praise God. Amen.

Sister Sandra Antonieta Morales Valenzuela, O.S.C.
Huehuetenango, Guatemala

"Never let the thought of Him leave your mind."   LEr 11B

Come Follow Me

Dancing was my greatest joy! When I heard the waltzes I could not keep my feet still, and the song, "I could have danced all night," was a great reality for me. But somehow amid the joy there was always a deep emptiness, an emptiness that slowly became more intense. The longing to become a Sister that had been within me since I was a very young child kept urging me and drawing me. My thoughts kept returning to my Franciscan uncle, who was such a man of prayer and peace. I wanted to become poor like him and give my life to Jesus; but how, where? I had never heard of the Poor Clares and would not know about them until many years later. Unknown to my family — there were twelve children — I used to find little hide-outs where I would pray and be so happy. When I was twelve, we moved to Canada, and my longing and my search continued on foreign soil; somehow I knew that the "where" would become clear.

During my working years I would spend long periods in church begging for light and, before I left, I always stopped by the large picture of our Mother of Perpetual Help, pouring out my heart to her. She had given a clear sign of her presence and an assurance that she would always be with us when our farm burned down in Holland during the Second World War. Everything, including the wallpaper on the wall behind her beautiful picture, was burnt, and yet her image itself remained untouched! It was she who guided me to the Poor Clares in Mission, British Columbia.

Dad, my sisters and I had watched a fifteen-minute television program on the Poor Clares about a year or so earlier, and it kept haunting me. At the suggestion of a priest, I went to visit them. It took three days by train. Arriving at the monastery, I rang the doorbell and stepped in, as the sign by the door suggested. Immediately I knew this was where Jesus was waiting for me. The same evening I was back on the train to return home, having filled out a form and asked to enter. Two days later I received a telegram saying I could come, and two weeks after that I was back on the train in order to enter.

Thirty-eight years have passed since that happy day, and I continue to be grateful each day for the gift of my vocation. The emptiness I once experienced has been filled to the greatest capacity with God's loving presence. Sometimes I want to climb a high mountain and shout, "If you want to be happy, give yourself completely to Jesus and let Him be your God, your Father, your Lover and your All."

My heart is full of gratitude: gratitude to God for choosing me from all eternity and looking upon His little one; gratitude to my dear parents, who had me baptized on the day I was born and who nourished this life of grace within me so that it could flower to the fulfillment of consecrated vows; gratitude for my brothers and sisters, with whom I shared the simple joys of life; gratitude for my community, who love me and support me; gratitude to our blessed and loving Mother for her protection, love and guidance and for bringing me here. May she continue to speak to the hearts of our young people today and draw many to consecrate themselves to her Son, Jesus.

Sister Mary Joanne Koot, O.S.C.
Mission, B.C., Canada

"...seeing the charity, humility and unity they have toward one another...."

TestCl 70

I Never Wanted To Be A Nun

When I was in middle and high school my plans were to marry and my dream was to become the first woman professional baseball player. When my great-aunt, a Sister of St. Francis, told me she'd pray for me to have a religious vocation, I thought that was the last thing I wanted to be!

From the first day of summer vacation I'd kick off my shoes, put on jeans and a tee shirt and spend my days roaming around the country, playing ball and many times spending time in quiet observation in creation. I loved the outdoors. My habit of going barefoot eventually was my introduction to the Poor Clares.

After I graduated from high school, I went to work as a nurse aide at St. Mary's Hospital in Rochester, Minn. After working a few months, I enrolled in the Rochester School of Vocational Nursing connected with St. Mary's Hospital. This program no longer exists. One of my classmates, Ellen, had a friend who had entered the Poor Clares. When she saw me going barefoot, she'd tease me that I should become a Poor Clare because they, too, went barefoot. This was the first time I heard of them but I thought that was kind of neat. Ellen's friend was Sr. Diane Ackerman. Later I would come to Korea with her. Our nursing school had some strict rules to protect their good name. One regulation forbids us to go to certain nightclubs or taverns. If we were caught going to these, we'd be expelled from school. One night I was out with some friends. They wanted to go to one of these off-limits nightclubs so I decided to go with them thinking, "Who would know?" Several days later, I was called to our school office where the Sister in charge wanted to see me. I knew why. I also knew this Sister was always trying to encourage us to go to the convent. So when she brought up the subject of where I had been, I just told her "Don't you know, I want to be a Sister?" I left her office not expelled but with an invitation to visit their convent. And yet I was caught by my own words. They kept going around in my mind.

After finishing nursing school, I went to work at the University of Minnesota Hospitals. I loved nursing and yet I didn't feel this was my lifelong vocation. In the hospital we are daily close to suffering and dying but also a renewal of life and healing. Still life seemed so fragile to me.

I decided to check out these funny Poor Clares that went barefoot. I couldn't see the Sister behind the black curtain when I first visited, but her voice and conversation seemed so normal and natural. How strange! Instead of being turned off by their strange life, I felt drawn.

At work in the hospital I would ponder how I wanted to spend the rest of my life. The answer in me was surprising not only to me but also to my family and friends. I wanted to live a hidden life of prayer. I asked to enter and was accepted on September 17, 1959.

Sometimes I've doubted my calling but I'm reminded, "You did not choose Me, but I chose you." This comforts me because despite all my faults and limitations, God is calling me each day anew. I still kick off my sandals and go barefoot when I can. I love the freedom that lets me do this.

Sister Madonna Winkels, O.S.C.
Cheju Island, Korea

"The Lord Himself has placed us not only as a form for others in being an example and mirror, but even for our sisters whom the Lord has called to our way of life as well that they in turn may be a mirror and example to those living in the world."

TestCl 19-20

A Beautiful Surprise from Our Loving God

"I have loved you with an everlasting love." Jeremiah 31:3

I was 28 years old and had a good-paying job, good friends, lots of money, a beautiful apartment and a car. I loved bowling and going to dances. Then something happened. I no longer wanted to do these things that I had enjoyed so much. Staying in my apartment was all I wanted to do. My girlfriends wanted to know what happened to me. Truly I wondered the same thing! My younger sister is a religious in an active order. Whenever she came for her home visit she would ask me if I wanted to come with her. My answer was always an emphatic, "I'll never be a nun."

One day, my mother was talking with one of our neighbors. I overheard her say that a young lady she knew wanted to be a Poor Clare. Her mother told her they were too strict and they were never allowed to come home. That is exactly what I needed to hear. That meant they didn't teach. I must have thought all nuns taught. For a long time I thought about this, wondering what the life of a Poor Clare was all about.

The priest I chose to talk to really discouraged me. He said I was too active, I would never see anyone, and I would never get to go home. After telling him my heart's desire and him trying so convincingly to discourage me, I almost lost my faith! I feel now that God led me to this priest to test my vocation. After this reaction, I tried to dismiss the whole idea from my mind. Then I became so restless; I went to church in the evenings and just cried, begging God to help me.

Finally I got the courage (grace?) to call the monastery and I was asked to come and talk to the abbess. It was a beautiful sunny day I picked for our visit. Before talking with Sister, I went to the extern Chapel. The quiet and beauty touched my heart! When I talked with the abbess I felt I was talking to a saint. She told me I could get my postulant dress ready. I hadn't told her my plans were top secret, and I didn't want anyone to know in case things didn't work out. To keep everything quiet, I asked the Sisters in Fremont to sew my postulant dress. They too wanted to know if this is what I really wanted, this kind of life. With no doubt in my mind, I assured them that it was. I remember how excited I was when they called to tell me the dress was finished. I kept it in the trunk of my car so no one would know about it.

About a month before entering, I told my girlfriends my plans. Needless to say, they too found it hard to believe. I also told my parents around that time. My dad told me to come home if I was not happy. My mom said I would be back.

My entrance date was set for September 8th. Filled with excited anticipation, I could hardly wait. The day finally arrived and as I walked to the door, I couldn't believe I was actually there. I rang the doorbell. The door opened wide and all of the Sisters were there to welcome me with open arms and hugs. I hadn't received so many hugs in all my life. After 43 years in the convent, I have never been happier. God is so good. I can never find words to thank Him enough for his beautiful loving surprise! "I have called you by name. You are mine." (Isaiah 43:1)

Sister M. Veronica Luebbert. O.S.C.
Omaha, Nebraska

"We are greatly bound to bless and praise God and be all the more strengthened to do good in the Lord."   *TestCl 22*

I Called You Before You Were Born

My mother was critically ill in hospital two months before I was born and she received the "Last" Sacraments. The priest who was administering this gift said to her: "If this baby lives, for sure it will be a priest if it is a boy, and a sister if it is a girl." St. Paul says in his letter to the Galatians: "...He who had set me apart before I was born and called me by his favor..." (1:15). Jeremiah says something similar: "...before you were born I dedicated you...." (1:5).

I did not live my life with the thought of fulfilling this prophecy. I was not even aware of it until much later, but there did indeed come a time when "...He...chose to reveal His Son to me...." (Galatians 1:16). Then the struggle began as I grappled with the meaning of Matthew's, "If a man wishes to come after me, he must deny his very self, take up his cross, and begin to follow in my footsteps" (16:24). It was at that very moment that my older sister, Doris, became critically ill after having given birth to her fourth little girl. I got on my knees and prayed to our Heavenly Father: "Lord, if someone has to die in our family, it should be me, for I have no husband or children." And addressing Our Lady I said: "Holy Mother, remember how Jesus needed you when He was a child, and my sister has a baby who needs her." My sister recovered and I got the grace to "deny my very self" and my dreams for the future and accept the call of a Poor Clare to prayer, for I realized at that moment that all I could do was pray.

Thirty years ago I entered with that intention and I continue to believe that God works His miracles through our asking. May He be praised for His loving providence that has so arranged things as to allow us to be "co-workers of God Himself" (St. Clare III Letter).

Sister Claire Marie Blondin, O.S.C.
Mission, B.C., Canada

"...Always persevere in holy poverty."   *TestCl*

River Of God's Love

The journey of faith that brought me to my vocation is like the experience of Ezekiel (Chapter 47:1-12) where Ezekiel is drawn by God into deeper and deeper water until he reaches the shore of peace and God's care for him.

As an eight-year-old child, I accompanied an elderly neighbor lady up the road to her Church and felt the warmth of Jesus' presence there as I had never experienced before. The memory of that warmth created in me a desire to find it again and I would seek it fervently as a young adult in various churches. I found this warmth in the Real Presence of Jesus in the Eucharist (I made my First Communion at the age of 21), and in prayer before the Blessed Sacrament.

The water of God's love was drawing me deeper and deeper. One day while volunteering in the church office a man said as he was leaving, "Thank you, Sister." I hastened to say that I was not a Sister. He turned around and looked at me with the most peaceful face I have ever seen, and said: "You should be a Sister." The waters were growing deeper. The man's words kept returning to my thoughts and in my prayer. Show me the way, Lord.

I began to pray about religious life and to look into religious communities. As a nurse, I initially looked at communities that provided nursing care. I felt great awe for the devotion and hard work of these Sisters, but was struck with how little time they had for prayer. Their care of the patients was indeed their prayer, but the waters were moving me elsewhere.

During this time, a Sister suggested that I look at contemplative communities. First I had to find out the meaning of that word. The waters of God's love were flowing still deeper and I discovered the Poor Clares about six miles from my apartment. I drove over and sat in the car, wrote down the address and went home to write to the sisters to ask about their life.

As I stepped into the Monastery, the warmth I first felt as an eight-year-old child flooded through me and I reached the shore of God's river of love and so the dance began:

> *From a distance*
> *I see the Trinity dancing,*
> *'Round and 'Round*
> *Love without beginning,*
> *Without end*
> *Love draws me, surrounds me*
> *Joy, peace, sorrow, suffering*
> *Fashion me*
> *Love, mercy, forgiveness, justice*
> *Bathe me*
> *Absorbed by the Trinity*

United in love
I am free to dance
The dance is love
The dance is peace
The dance is God's dwelling in me
Me dwelling in God
Now and for eternity we dance.

How can I repay the Lord for His goodness to me? The cup of salvation I will take up. I will call on the name of the Lord. My vows to the Lord I will fulfill before all His people (Psalm 116:10-19).

With St. Clare I look on my Crucified Lord, and "behold Him, consider Him, contemplate Him and desire to imitate Him. If you suffer with Him, you shall reign with Him. If you weep with Him, you will rejoice with Him. If you die with Him on the Cross of Sorrow, you shall possess heavenly mansions in the brightness of the saints, and your name in the Book of Life shall be called Glorious." (2nd Letter to Agnes 20-21).

Blessed are you O Lord who has created me! (Process of Canonization of St. Clare 14, 9).

Sister M. Veronica, O.S.C.
Jamaica Plain, Massachusetts

"...how blessed are those to whom it has been given to walk this way and to persevere till the end!"   *TestCl 73*

Clare's Bright Light

I lived on the southern tip of Jeju Island. In 1981 I volunteered as a Sunday school teacher for our parish. On Vocation Sunday of that year I took our young Mass servers to a convent on our island. At that time I didn't know anything about the convent there except it was a place where only special women entered.

Later, I came to the Isidore Nursing Home to visit with some friends. Before going home we decided to visit this convent. Sr. Frances Kwon met us and gave us a speech I will never forget. She said people living in the world had much different problems than those living in the monastery. Most people's main concern and problems were how to get ahead, how to advance in study or business, or how to have a good marriage. The Sisters' problems were much simpler. For example, a short Sister cannot reach high places so must ask a tall Sister for help. The tall Sister is always being asked to do this and do that and feels she is being used. Coming to know ourselves in humility and accepting each other as sisters was our challenge. That is when I realized they are just like us.

I wanted to enter the Carmelite Monastery in Busan so I was visiting them and writing letters back and forth. Since they lived on the Mainland of Korea and I lived on an island, going there was not easy, so I asked Sr. Frances to direct me in my vocation. I was preparing to enter the Carmelites in September of 1984 but something was very wrong. I felt very sad instead of happy. My heart was in darkness and so heavy with burden. I just could not make the necessary preparations to enter.

On Pentecost on my way to evening Mass, my heart was in great pain. I thought: This must not be my vocation after all. I was not called to be a contemplative. I will get married. Suddenly on the bus a bright shining light surrounded me. In that light I knew I was called to be a Poor Clare. It was the brightness of St. Clare. I became very happy. The next day I called Sr. Frances to ask to talk with her.

While on retreat at the monastery before entering, I saw Sr. Madonna wearing blue jeans, carrying a shovel and followed by a big dog. That confirmed for me my calling. The life here struck me as being one of love, freedom, brightness and liberty to dress in whatever clothes were needed for the occasion.

Prayer is the foundation of my life dedicated to God. This brings about freedom, love and light. I entered the monastery on February 2, 1985.

Sister Juliana Kang, O.S.C.
Jeju Island, Korea

"The form of life of the order of the Poor Sisters...is to observe the Holy Gospel of our Lord Jesus Christ...."　　　　RCl 1,2

In The End, It's All About Love

In the beginning and in the end, it's all about love. I was a teenager when I fell in love — a head-over-heels, I-want-to-be-with-you-all-the-time kind of love. I knew it was the real deal. It's not that I hadn't been "in love" before that. I had "fallen" for my first boyfriend Timmy in kindergarten, and he remained special to me all through my growing-up years and beyond. But this...this was different. This love was total **gift**, and it invited me to be gift in turn. This lover was the Lord.

How was I to respond to such an invitation? My heart was led in many directions as I got to know my gifts and interests. I enjoyed tutoring, and I had a great love of scientific research. Missionary work also captivated me. Teacher, scientist, missionary, or some combination of the above? That was my dilemma. I took my questions to prayer. Gradually, I was drawn more and more to the contemplative life, and I came to understand that this call encompassed all of these apostolates and more within the ministry of prayer. My interest in so many areas was giving me a taste for a call to serve the whole Body of Christ through the contemplative life. I didn't have to decide between interests. Like St. Therese of Lisieux I would choose them all through a life of prayer at the heart of the Church.

Once this was clear, it was not long before I dropped out of college and dropped into the monastery. A major discovery during my time of formation was that one does not "become" a Franciscan. I had had a Franciscan heart all along, and the formation process simply revealed it to me. I was home.

Another discovery I made upon entering the community was that I truly had sisters. I had two brothers but no sisters growing up, so this was a new reality for me. Through this experience I have come to treasure not only my monastery community but also the whole reality of our worldwide Franciscan family. God gives us as sisters and brothers to each other as instruments of His Word and as support along the pilgrim path.

When I began my journey I had a strong romantic streak, and I still have a tendency to this today. My idealism crashed headlong with the human condition, which I found (and still sometimes find) difficult to accept in myself and others. I expected deep prayer and love of God, loving sisters all working, praying and playing in harmony. I expected crosses, too, but that was seen through a bit of a rosy glow. All of these expectations proved true, but the passage of time and experience has filtered these expectations through real life. I have a greater knowledge and acceptance of my inner weaknesses, and I think that my perception of others has been tempered with compassion.

Some years of living the contemplative life have given me a comfort and ease with the life in one sense. Yet, there is always the challenge of a new call each new day to new life. There is always a danger of no longer expecting great things to happen in the face of daily life and its struggles. The cross has often not been found in the great dramatic moments of life, but in the acceptance of the things that come my way each day. I am challenged not to be complacent, but to keep expecting the Lord to do great things while doing my best in the dailyness. I could get trapped by the status quo. I could get disturbed unduly by some events in the Church and the world around me, or by my own lack of zeal. I find myself, however, called to an open-ended **hope**. I look forward to the future. I have no idea what it will bring, but I have a sense of trust that God is working great things in us if we let Him.

How do I envision this future? I dream of a community that continues to be vibrant with life. I see people who enjoy being and sharing with each other on many levels. I see a community on fire with love for God, respectful of each other, not afraid of facing the unknown or of trying new ways of living our contemplative ideal... people open to the future and to growth. I see a community that is poor and simple, realistic about mundane realities and yet trusting in God's providence. More than all, I see a community of **joy** and **love**.

Sister Charlene Toups, O.S.C.
New Orleans, Louisiana

"...to live in obedience, without anything of our own, and in chastity." RCl:2

Dwelling in the Father's Love

When I think back on my vocation as a Poor Clare, two books were special instruments of God's grace to me. The first one was *The Way of Perfection* by St. Teresa of Avila. For St. Teresa, living in God was her only happiness, and that came from her absolute trust in Him, which enabled her to cut off all the things in life that were unnecessary. I felt such an attraction to this in my heart, that after reading the book, I couldn't even sleep at night! I thought, "I, too, want to live that way!" Then I came across Henri Nouwen's *Genessee Diary*. In it, he shared the ordinary day by day life of the monks living for God. I thought how great it would be if I, too, could have the chance to live this kind of contemplative life! However, at 45 years old, I was already older than most communities would accept, and also thought I was lacking in other requirements, like a higher educational background.

At this time I had already been a professed member of the Secular Franciscan Order for more than 10 years, and worked at the Franciscan Friary. A younger friend of mine was a novice at the Poor Clare Monastery in Jeju, and I attended Sister Cecilia's first profession. After the ceremony, when we were visiting with some of the sisters in the parlor, the novice directress, Sister Frances, threw out to me an unexpected question: "Monica, how about you coming here? Of course, the friars would be disappointed in losing you!" It was like she had somehow discovered the secret desire in my heart! I was so happy, but also afraid. What if I tried and couldn't succeed? So I didn't give her any answer, but just laughed! I didn't even share this with the Franciscan priest and brother that I was travelling with by plane. But when I got home, I was so happy that I phoned my brother and his wife to tell them this news, which seemed like a miracle to me! At the time, my family didn't seem too happy about my desire to be a sister! Secretly, to prepare myself for the gift of a contemplative vocation, I had been living apart from my family, as a practice in independence. Also, I had started to attend classes at the Catechetical Institute in Seoul, to deepen my theological knowledge. I told my family that this, for me, would be the path to happiness - a possibility for new life had opened, and that is what I wanted to choose, if it would be possible!

So as not to lose this precious gift, while still working, I made a month retreat (half-day retreat and half-day work) and attended daily Mass. At this time, a book about Abraham's faith by Cardinal Martini was a grace for me. I read about how Abraham responded in faith to God, and I was given greater confidence to follow the Lord! Then, in the summer, three of the Poor Clares from Jeju attended a Franciscan seminar in Seoul. Since I was a Secular Franciscan, I also attended, and spent a lot of time with the sisters. We became very close, and I sensed that their hearts were open to me in regard to the possibility of my vocation with them. So I went to Jeju to make a retreat, and expressed the desire that was in my heart.

So, within the next year, I entered the monastery, and experienced that I had found what my heart was so deeply seeking! This was truly the path to happiness! Living in community with the sisters, I feel something like a mother in a family. This is truly home for me! I experience this "at-homeness" especially in the presence of the Blessed Sacrament during adoration, and also in reading good books. If I were married, with a husband and children, I would like to keep the house neat and clean and prepare delicious food on beautiful dishes. During any leisure, I would love to read books, through which I gain so much! For children, when they come home from school and call out, "Mom!" and mother answers, they are assured and happy. I feel the same way at prayer, especially in the presence of the Blessed Sacrament, where I experience such peace — just like a child, assured in her mother's presence! That is happiness! I give all this happiness to the Lord, for Him to keep, asking Him to remind me of it, and give it back to me when I need it the most. Even when I am anxious, and difficult things happen, peace is restored to my heart.

I am so grateful for my community, who have accepted me just as I am. No matter what hardships or sorrows come, I have been able to live because of the love of my sisters. Even when I make mistakes, I am not ashamed because I trust that I can ask and receive forgiveness. Through my weaknesses I also experience my need for the sisters. This is my poverty, and an important aspect of the spirituality of St. Clare, who tells us that only the poor can inherit the Kingdom of Heaven. Jesus came to this earth and lived among us, and I experience this deeply. Sometimes I want to run from my wounds or the dark places within me, but I find that when I give them to the Lord, not clinging to them as my own possession, I receive new healing. When I accept myself, who was once "lost," I feel myself become a new creation and am given new life, which is so good and precious, and something that pleases God!

Sister Monica (Kyong-Suk) Kim, O.S.C.
Yang Yang Community
(A new Poor Clare foundation in Korea)

"Know your vocation."   *TestCl 4*

Laughter Behind The Grille

The oldest of a family of eight children, I was raised in Yakima, Washington, and received twelve years of Catholic education.

I experienced an early desire to love God (as St. Therese did) which grew into a desire for the religious life. By the end of the eighth grade, I was firmly settled in the intention of becoming a cloistered Poor Clare Nun. The specific attraction to the Poor Clare Order came through a phrase written in a diocesan newspaper, "laughter floating out from behind the grille." It was the joy of the Poor Clares that attracted me to their life!

The time of my entrance (1966) was just after the conclusion of the Second Vatican Council, and all the changes were starting! The first years were exciting as the habits and names of the sisters were changed, the liturgy adapted, the house renovated and numerous customs adapted — all with charity as the guiding principle.

I participated in many facets of the work of the community, and was the sacristan for more than 20 years. I am now going into my twelfth year as community cook, a very satisfying job for me. I try to live united with God throughout the day and to desire above all else to have "the spirit of the Lord and its holy activity."

Sister Rita Louise McLean, O.S.C.
Spokane, Washington

"...I (Francis) ask and counsel you, my ladies, to live always in this most holy life and poverty."
RCl 6:7

From the sandy beaches of Santa Cruz to the Delmonte tomato cannery west of East 14th Street, Oakland: This is my vocation story.

Growing up in paradise presents a special problem for the rest of one's life: one always regrets having to leave. Santa Cruz is "where the kneeling mountains meet the praying seas," as the Franciscans like to say about their California missions. A few years ago I went to a reunion of school-mates from Holy Cross, our parochial school run by the Adrian Dominicans in Santa Cruz. Most of my school friends had stayed right there in Santa Cruz, some still working on the boardwalk.

If I look for the factors that propelled my family to relocate from Santa Cruz, where my mother and I were born (both delivered by the same Doctor Dowling, M.D.) and my father was assistant chief of police, to the city of Oakland, I would have to name International Communism and local politics. My father was fascinated by communism and was becoming a self taught expert on the subject. At the same time he had made enemies in our town during his 16 years on the Police Force. When the district attorney of Alameda County offered Dad a position as chief inspector with his own office and staff, answerable only to the D.A., it was the perfect career move. His job was to collaborate with the other intelligence officers in the Bay Area, from the FBI, CIA and independent intelligence agencies. My mom went along with courage, my brother was too young to care, and I stifled my anguish and desolation.

So it was that I began the latter third of my freshman year at Oakland High. I had gone from a school of 120, where all of the boys suited up for the football team and the girls carried the down box and the ten-yard markers, to a school of 2000. There was no prayer before class, no crucifixes, nuns, daily mass. It was gray and boring. I remember being attracted by the Jewish kids, but they would not let me into their group. I became friends with a Greek Orthodox girl and a Protestant whom I attempted to convert. Every night I would cry myself to sleep. This was a bleak time in my life.

Somehow I found my way to a little library run by Third Order Franciscans down near East 14th Street and the afore-mentioned tomato factory. It is said that the sense of smell is the most primitive and evocative of memory. An over-cast day with the smell of tomatoes being processed is my image of the Dark Night. God, who is not want to leave his petitioners without recourse, came to my aid in the persons of these dear lay Franciscans. They let me borrow books and talked with me about holy topics and best of all point-ed across the street from their library to St. Elizabeth's High School where even on Saturdays I could see boys hanging out the windows as they put in their "detention" time.

In the fall my precious Baptist mom went with me to register for my sophomore year at SE. The Franciscan Friars were our teachers and friends. I and a few others in our sophomore class immediately started a Junior Third Order with the young friars as our formation directors. The school play that year was "Song of Bernadette." I got the leading role. Life was definitely on the upswing. SE was not big on the intellectual side of life but was great for drama, glee club and public speaking. We also had the best Friday night dances in the Bay Area. Three years go by quickly when one is having fun. However, we were required to graduate and move on, as hard as that seemed.

I believe it was the experience of moving from Santa Cruz to Oakland that gave me the inner resolve to invest my life with God among the Poor Clares of Santa Barbara. Gertrude Stein was supposed to have said of Oakland, California, "There is no there, there." What I found was that God was there for me, and if in Oakland, then anywhere. I need not fear moving on because God could find me any place and everywhere.

Sister Beth Lynn, O.S.C.
Minneapolis, Minnesota

"...all are bound to serve and provide for their sisters who are ill...."

RCl 8:14

Locked Door — Lost Key

May 1941: With a determined look and firm jaw the Mother Superior said, "Novice Agnes, you do not have a vocation, never did. Pack your clothes and go home."

My young mind raced back to my sophomore year when I studied the *Baltimore Catechism* under the supervision of a Benedictine Sister. She had invited me to make a retreat at their Motherhouse. As a result of doing that, my life changed. From that day forward my desire to serve God as a religious grew. The following year I entered as an Aspirant/Postulant, then received the white veil and habit of a novice. Within a period of three years my health failed and with it the straw that broke the camel's back: I broke a strict, forbidden rule, thus the command to leave. I departed quickly, closed the door, and threw away the key. End of Chapter, never looked back.

The future beckoned and the possibilities were numerous with school and work. My spirituality dissolved with the lock and key, but not entirely. It consisted of Sunday Mass and Holy Communion and an extremely rare thought of God in between. World War II also changed my Life. War and the thoughts of death had a strange effect on young people. I met and married a Catholic soldier. Five children were conceived in this union. Two died at birth. The three survivors are the oldest daughter with children into the fourth generation; the middle daughter who became a School Sister of Notre Dame and the youngest, son, self-employed.

Time passed but our marriage had already started to crumble, inch by inch. Now was the time for help but I did not open the door. Amid the turmoil I had little room in my heart for God.

1950: Inspired by a higher being of which I was unaware, I removed a stationery box from its secret place, opened the lid, took out a book of prayers that I had saved from convent days and read a few paragraphs. Along with this I rediscovered the written treasures in the *Imitation of Christ*. Without my knowledge, the Holy Spirit was slowly breaking the barrier to get me back on track. He was about the Father's work.

1957: Lent. Inspired by homilies from Sunday Mass, I made a decision to attend daily Mass. Along with much criticism and opposition I kept my resolution faithfully. Lent ended and the desire for daily Mass was strong, stronger than a two-edged sword. Once again, braving religious harassment and verbal cruelty, I was allowed to fulfill my heart's desire. This had to be the real turning point: God showed me the entrance to His inner chamber. At the crossroads I knew in my heart that I had a choice to make and could not have both; one road led to alcohol, dancing and immoral conduct; the other choice was the Cross and

Jesus. I silently chose the Cross and from that day forward my spiritual life would *never, ever* be the same.

1968: Twenty-five years of religious persecution and now freedom. My spouse walked out, bag and baggage for greener pastures. Minus the obstacles, my inner life grew by leaps and bounds under the guidance of an experienced priest director.

1977: One day Father suggested I enter a convent. My reply, "No, I'm too old." Like St. Peter, I denied His request three times. I lived in the solitude of my home, perhaps a hermit. God was good. He led me into the desert, spoke to my heart and allured me with sweet meats. Little by little He closed the gate until I could no longer escape His embrace. He is a jealous God.

1978: I woke up spiritually and knew beyond a doubt that God had a plan for me in religious life. One evening during prayer in my living room, I saw an image of Jesus on the Cross with one arm embracing St. Francis. I did not know what it meant since I had not experienced such events previously. Before Mass that same evening I knelt close to the communion rail, looked at Jesus on the Cross above the altar and the same image returned. I knew this was Franciscan. There were Franciscan Poor Clare Nuns just outside the city. I called the Monastery for information. Two phone calls and many visits assured me that God had directed me to a house of prayer and contemplation. In due time I was accepted and entered the cloister on May 1, 1979 at the age of 57.

During my Solemn Profession ceremony, August 10, 1985, the reality of my vocation came to true light: I had found the Lost Key and unlocked the Door.

Sister Mary Joseph Palacios, O.S.C.
Brenham, Texas

"...be very careful... to not at any time turn from the path of the Lord through our own fault, negligence or ignorance." TestCl 74

How Good God Is!

As I look back on my life, I experience the deep providence of God. I'm now 70 years old and have lived religious life 29 years. If you count my time in waiting for the Monastery to be built here so I could enter, it would be 34 years.

When I was three years old, I contracted the measles. Many children catch this disease and recover, but some do not. At the time in Korea we did not have medicine for this, and my recovery was considered impossible. I was dying. My family did not have any religion but a friend of my grandmother was a Catholic. She asked if she could baptize me since I was dying. Permission was given and I was named Maria. Miracle of miracles, here I am still living! I not only survived the measles but I also survived two big wars and living the life of a refugee for some time.

I grew up not knowing I had been baptized and became the age when young women marry. This is a very important time for a Korean woman. My family, friends, and neighbors were all involved in trying to find a good match for me. Of all the people around me, I was the most concerned. The friend of my grandmother who baptized me came to visit me. She was worried I'd marry outside the church. She took me to church and explained to the priest and me how she had baptized me. So at the age of 23, after studying the Catechism, I was formally baptized at Christmas. The young woman teaching us the Catechism had been in a convent but had to leave because of ill health. There was still something special about her though and this started me thinking of religious life. I thought that would be the best thing in the world but I felt I would not qualify. I would have to marry. So to prepare for marriage, I started taking sewing and cooking classes. I was seeing how beautiful marriage life could be where two people love and cherish each other for all eternity.

My faith really wasn't very deep. I started to read the Gospels. One day as I read Luke's Gospel chapter 20:27-40, it changed my whole way of thinking about marriage. In heaven, there is no marrying, but we live as angels. This shocked me at the time. After this I wanted very much to offer my life to God. Jesus said, "I came to serve and not to be served," so through sewing and cooking classes, I looked for ways to serve.

In my life, I learned that God uses all that has gone before us as an instrument to lead us to our goal. I can only give thanks and praise to God. Nothing can compare with God's love.

In 1969 one day in the Catholic paper there was an article about the Poor Clares starting in Korea. I received the Catholic paper in the morning before going to work so I just laid it on the table. When I came back from work, the article about the Poor Clares just jumped out at me. In the paper were the name and address of the Sisters. I went to see them. Joining their Monastery was my only hope after that. I was 35 years old and had to wait five years before entering in 1974. The sewing and cooking classes I attended to prepare for marriage I now use to serve in the Monastery. Also, my family have all become Catholic except my elder sister but her husband was baptized on his deathbed. How good God is to all!

Sister Margaret Kim, O.S.C.
Jeju Island, Korea

"I admonish and exhort all my sisters...to strive always to imitate the way of holy simplicity, humility and poverty and to preserve the integrity of our holy way of living."   TestCl 56

The Evangelical Life of Saint Clare

Faithful For Forty Years

Pope Innocent had approved Clare's gospel project at the end of her life. It was another pope, Gregory IX, who most severely tested Clare and her form of life. Gregory was desirous of bringing all of the independent groups of the women's poverty movement into one rule written under the auspices of Gregory. In 1219 he began encouraging women's groups to accept his "Form and Manner of Living for the poor cloistered nuns of Tuscany and Lombardy." The Benedictine form of monasticism was a keystone of this rule that prohibited the nuns from leaving the cloister except to found a new monastery of the same Order. This was a papal effort to reform religious life for women.

Gregory's project was different than the project of Francis and Clare. From 1212, the beginning of the poor sisters community at San Damiano, until 1228, the defining first 16 years of their Charism, the sisters followed the rule of Francis and the friars with necessary adaptations for a women's group. Francis died in 1226 and was canonized in 1228. Pope Gregory IX commissioned the friar, Thomas of Celano, to write a life of Francis. Clare is eulogized in this first life of Francis as if she were already dead and canonized. Clare was just 34 years old and would live another 26 years. It was at this time that Gregory was intensifying his campaign to gather all of the women's groups into what he had begun to call the Order of St. Damian. It seems fair to say that the pope was using Clare and the community at San Damiano in Assisi to sell his product, namely his Rule of Gregory. The biographer of Pope Gregory actually claims that Gregory founded the poor sisters of San Damiano. That could be true. The Pope, however, did not found the community that lived at San Damiano in Assisi.

For forty years Clare remained faithful to her God-given vocation. She never wavered or doubted her call. In her Testament Clare wrote: "The Son of God has been made for us the Way, which our blessed Father Francis, his true lover and imitator has shown us by word and example." After Francis' death, Clare was the strong and loving support to his first companions. It was these same friars, Leo, Juniper, and Angelo who gathered around her bed as she lay dying....

His Grace is Sufficient For Me

His grace is sufficient for everyone...

Opening the Door of My Heart

A great artist once painted a picture depicting Christ standing at the door of a house knocking, and this door had no latch or doorknob. That door represents my heart and the knocking was the grace of Jesus inviting me into His heart. He penetrated my heart and moved me to invite Him in.

There is no hour in the life of a person comparable to that hour when Jesus Christ comes knocking at the door of their heart. During my high school days I had plans to enter nursing school after graduation, to marry and to have several children. I recall telling one of the priests in our parish that I'd never want to be a nun because I liked the boys so much. About two years after this statement I began to feel a pull in the direction of religious life.

I was working as a junior aide at Nazareth Hospital in Philadelphia and felt such an admiration for the sisters there who cared for the sick. The same community of sisters taught at Nazareth Academy, my high school. Here too their prayerfulness and dedication moved me. I know God, who was inviting me into His heart, put this attraction there. I loved skating and dancing and my attraction to the boys had not diminished; yet I felt pulled in another direction and tried to resist it. Our God is a jealous lover and He was very persistent. After much resisting I felt the attraction growing and began to see myself as a religious sister bringing Christ's care to the sick. I also felt a strong attraction to the foreign missions.

I knew God would show me the way. One day while in the library I was handed a book which I opened to a page telling about the Sisters of St. Clare. Although these sisters had a monastery in Philadelphia I had never heard of them. At that moment I knew I wanted to learn more about them and wrote to them. I soon received a warm response inviting me to come and visit. The sisters were cloistered contemplative nuns, and I was surprised to find them so full of life and joy and looked forward to visiting them on other occasions. These were ordinary women living an extraordinary life for Christ and I knew I wanted to do the same.

When I told my parents of my leanings, my dad was disappointed at first; he said he would rather see me in an active congregation. At that time he and mom confided in me that for years they had prayed together that one of their children would have a religious vocation. They later visited the sisters at the monastery, and this had a positive effect. Gone were their hesitations. They wanted me to be happy and suspected I would be—and anyway, it was my choice.

By the time I graduated from high school I knew I wanted to enter the Poor Clares. I also wanted to make the most of that last summer with parties and dancing, trips to the shore, etc., all the time knowing that there was more to discover in life.

The night before my entrance I was up most of the night dancing. My parents took me to a nightclub because my Dad wanted to have the last dance with his daughter. We danced and danced until the place closed and then we went to a bar nearby with a dance floor in back and were there until it closed. I guess he didn't want the night to end and neither did I.

The next afternoon I entered the monastery after having a festive dinner with all my family. The sisters were also having a day of celebration because it was the Feast of St. Francis. One thing that stands out in my mind after all these years was that after spending the afternoon with them I was so happy to be shown my cell with its straw bed. That straw mattress felt so good because I was so tired and longed to put my head down. I had no problem sleeping that first night or any other.

During those early days I heard "a good Poor Clare is one who eats well, sleeps well and prays well." I had no trouble with the first two but had much to learn about praying well. One's first years in a monastery are days of learning about the life of prayer and living and growing in communion with God and your sisters. I'm grateful for these early formative years although they were sometimes difficult. When it came time I freely chose to vow obedience, live without anything of my own, in chastity and in enclosure—obviously not knowing all that would be asked of me and trusting in God's grace.

The years after Vatican II were a painful time in the community. We were asked to look at questions regarding renewal, and some sisters did not welcome any renewal. These questions caused me to rethink many things that I just accepted as part of the Clare life. I desired some changes and sought them in another Poor Clare Community.

Ten years after entering the community in Philadelphia I requested a transfer to the Monastery in Greenville, South Carolina, where I felt I'd have a deeper prayer life and find a broader vision regarding enclosure. This transfer was a blessing. I was twenty-eight and rediscovering myself, my gifts, bonding with my sisters and forming deep friendships. I was called forth to different forms of service within this community and through the years held many positions and responsibilities. In the Clare life every job is important and equal because it is done for the love of the Lord. Each sister does her part so that all have the time and leisure for contemplation.

Enclosure has not always been easy. In looking back I feel living an enclosed life or living in a limited space widens my vision so that I can identify with limits of others: those who are sick, out of work, disabled, shut in, and those who are living in abusive situations. These are the people I lift up in my prayer. Living enclosed is an emptying that transforms and frees me to be before the Lord and dance to the stirrings of the Divine in my life.

A Poor Clare is first and foremost a woman of prayer. She is one who has been touched by God's love so intimately that she desires to surrender herself to Him through a life of love and contemplation. Her life of prayer is a continual search to know God and this enables her to enter deeply into the lives of her brothers and sisters with all their pain and joy. My dancing today is following in the footsteps of Christ and with Him lifting up the needs of the entire human family to God our Father. This is my priesthood.

I am a Clare today because of the grace of God who has gifted me with a special vocation. I do not merit such a calling. It is gift.

Sister Maryann Jenkins, O.S.C.
Greenville, South Carolina

"Let the Sisters, to whom the Lord has given the grace of working, work faithfully and devotedly..."   RCl 7

A Gift, A Grace

Celebrating my Silver Jubilee of Profession of Vows as a Poor Clare in 2002 brought me back to that first moment when the whole spiritual world seemed to have flung open its doors before me so that I might explore it.

One afternoon, in my first year in high school, I went to the school library to borrow one of the books in the Nancy Drew series. As I looked at the shelves, there was not a single copy there. Leaving the library in frustration, I grabbed a book without even reading the title and checked it out. Then I started reading the book, *The Life of Saint Catherine of Siena* by Raymond Capua. It was the first time I was exposed to the knowledge that there was such a thing as a personal relationship with God and that it was possible here on earth. That kind of relationship fascinated me. At that time I did not know what meditation was and/or how to go about it, but somehow, reading the book and thinking about what I had read, led me without my knowing it into meditation.

At times I found myself questioning Jesus before the Blessed Sacrament. The days following that experience made my daily Mass participation more meaningful and our annual retreats deepened my desire to know more about God: that He had sent His own Son, Jesus, to be like us and to die on the Cross that I might share in His own life and love was so compelling. I began to admire the saints and all those who have dedicated themselves to God as priests and religious. Toward the end of high school, entering into a deep and personal relationship with God was the only thing that I was yearning and thirsting for. I could not see myself entering into that kind of relationship with God without leaving everything behind and becoming a religious.

After high school, my parents gave me a choice to pursue a career in *sciences or to stay put at home.* To pursue a career was meaningless to me as a degree was the last thing I wanted. However, I thought of my parents and how unhappy they would be if I were to say no to their request. I thought then of accepting their offer and made up my mind to pursue religious life after finishing the course. Each day, from the time I enrolled in the university, part of my daily prayer was to beg God for the grace of a vocation. I remember one day saying, *God, I would be happy to be anything as long as I was a religious.* As the years went by I became more convinced that I could not possibly be happy as an active religious. I felt that I was already living an active religious life by being a daily Mass-goer and by my activity in the parish as a member of the Legion of Mary in the Philippines. This involved teaching catechism and preparing candidates to receive the sacraments, especially adult baptism, confirmation and matrimony for couples who wanted their marriage regularized. The lifestyle of active religious at the time that I was discerning my vocation did not warrant much of a change for me. I felt a need to leave everything behind in order to enter into that kind of relationship with God that I desired.

At this point I began to look at the different contemplative communities in the Philippines. It was at this time also that my papers for emigrating to Canada came so I said to myself: *Well, if God still wants me, it does not matter where I am or where I will be. If He is calling me, the call will always be there.* With that conviction I had my papers processed for emigrating to Canada. I thought that in two years I would have traveled as much as I wanted and then I could go back to the Philippines and enter a monastery. This plan to enter a monastery in the Philippines was my most guarded secret.

The first year I was in Canada brought news of my father's terminal illness so I decided to stay. I knew that my life would not be the same once I went back to the Philippines, having lost my mother in my late teens. Besides, most of my friends had themselves emigrated to North America. The second year of my life here in North America compelled me to look into religious life seriously. I went to see our assistant pastor, a young priest, who became my spiritual director. There were moments when I did not quite agree with some of the things that he asked me to do during the whole discernment period; yet I had to believe that God was guiding me through him. I followed his advice and visited different active religious communities in the archdiocese. Meanwhile, I kept telling him that I was drawn to a contemplative life. One day, after spending a day with one of the several active religious communities he suggested, I was so exasperated that I went to see him right away! I told him that I was not drawn to any of the communities he suggested, that I was finished with the search and that I would go on with my life because I had done all that I could with no positive results. Upon hearing that, he told me to contact the Poor Clares. I asked him, *how, write them?* He said, *no, phone them!* That evening, I phoned the Poor Clares. I was interviewed on the phone and was asked to come for a visit. The weekend was the only time I was free; so that Sunday, I went to see the Mission Poor Clares. As soon as I walked in, I felt that I had come home. The following week, I was back to Mission to spend a weekend. I felt so drawn to this life that I begged for admission before I left.

The last two weeks before my entrance date were hard for me as I had to face the thousand questions that my family, relatives and friends asked. The love relationship burning within me made me strong enough to face all the seemingly legitimate reasons they gave for me not to enter a monastery to serve God. They said that I could serve God in different apostolates, that it was not necessary to be a cloistered contemplative. The conviction that I would not be at peace if I did not try the life was the only answer I could give them.

Another struggle I went through prior to my entrance was to give up my job. In one of my interviews with the Abbess, she pointed out that I was new in the country, that I had no other security except my job. *Was I willing to give that up?* At that time, I believed that if I gave up my job to seek His will, surely He would see to it that if this community were not for me, I would be able to find a job. However, I did not have the courage to quit my job. I stayed up all night asking God to give me the grace to give up whatever I was attached to. In my struggle, I realized it was not the job I was hanging on to but the people I worked with. The following morning, back at work, as soon as I quit my job, I felt a big heavy load fall off my shoulders. I realized that a call is a gift, a grace, and so is the ability to respond.

Sister Mary Francis Macaballug, O.S.C.
Alexandria, Ontario, Canada

"She (Clare) considered that the most precious pearl of heavenly desire which she purchased by selling everything, could not be possessed with the gnawing concern for temporal things."
LegCl 13e

Touched (Or Rather Shoved) By God

I had always felt the same way about the word "cloister" that King Herod felt about John the Baptist. "When he had heard him speak he was greatly perplexed and yet he liked to listen to him" (Mark 6:20). At about the age of eight years old, I remember feeling some attraction to the idea of cloister. Remaining perplexed this continued until I entered the Spokane Poor Clares at twenty-four years of age. Part of the perplexity stemmed from the fact that I grew up on a several thousand acre ranch in the middle of Montana and wasn't all that ready to give up my independence.

God started nudging me a little more firmly in college. I wrote to several orders but it only added to my perplexity. I was attracted to the Franciscan Friars but didn't know too much about the Poor Clares. I joined the Secular Franciscans as a candidate while a junior in college which helped to ease some of this internal pressure. Upon graduation I prepared to start my internship in Spokane, Washington to become a certified Medical Technologist and was also trying to figure out how to combine the secular with the religious.

God wasn't letting up on me so I looked up the Spokane Diocese in The Catholic Directory to see if there was a fraternity of Secular Franciscans. Much to my surprise, not only were there Secular Franciscans but also a monastery of Poor Clares. I decided to write to the Poor Clares and find out what they were like. God was working behind the scenes in other areas also, as I had an apartment ready and waiting for me in Spokane. After arriving in Spokane and starting internship, I made an appointment to visit the Poor Clares on Labor Day weekend. The morning of the appointment, I went out to start the car and nothing. It was dead! Panicking, I immediately called Dad. He said, "Did you look under the hood?" I was embarrassed but answered, "No." Hanging up and investigating under the car hood, I found that someone had been halfway along with stealing my car battery and was interrupted. That gave me a clue that possibly the powers of evil weren't too happy about my going to visit the sisters.

The visit went well and I kept in contact with them. They patiently prayed for all my tests and I, in return, bothered them with more phone calls. I also was investigating various active congregations in the area. It was very satisfying to have a full appointment book but unfortunately it did help to confuse the issue, even though I didn't realize it. I thought I was trying to be circumspect but actually, I was trying to avoid God's nudging me in the direction of the Poor Clares. The idea of cloister still was very scary to me.

Finally, God gave me a shove. I was meeting with the vocation directress of the congregation in which I was very interested. We were having a very heartfelt discussion on discernment when we both felt a very strong feeling that I should be a Poor Clare nun. I had the sense of a being of light in the room, but couldn't actually see it. The directress seemed to sense something as well and we both quickly came to the conclusion that I belonged with the Poor Clares. I don't know what her reaction was to the experience, but I was left with a profound sense of peace.

I visited the Poor Clares for a few days over the Christmas break and felt very much at home. In fact, I was ready to quit internship and sign up. However, the directress of formation said, "No, one needs to finish as it is important to have the sense of completion." So unwillingly, I went back and finished internship.

Throughout the rest of the year of internship, I continued to argue with myself about joining the Poor Clares, but the sense of peace deep within me never left. I did pass my boards and was ready to ask for the papers for admittance into the order. I entered the Spokane Poor Clares on November 11, 1987, and was quite at peace with the idea of cloister.

Sister Colleen Byrne, O.S.C.
Spokane, Washington

"...her speech was always about things of God."　　　　　*Proc 2:10*

Adsum — Here I Am

The invitation was at first faint, yet persistent. I felt lured to solitude. Soon it became a reality. For five weeks a one-room hermitage atop a high desert mesa in Arizona would be my place of solitude where God would grant audience to my solitary soul. I thought I was fully ready for this experience but was soon to discover otherwise.

I left my beloved community who supported me in this spiritual venture, little realizing that they would never for one moment leave my heart or my consciousness. They are a tremendous source of love and joy and leaving them behind for even five weeks was more painful that I could have imagined.

I arrived at my hermitage without books, tapes, CD's or anything that would distract me from my purpose of total solitude and listening to God. I had food and clothes and an idealism that was soon shattered. The name of my hermitage was ADSUM (Here I Am). I was struck by its appropriateness as my prayer for the past few months was that I be given the grace to be totally available to God during my stay here. So here I was...alone...totally alone with only the silence of the surrounding hills and the whisper of the desert wind. It was an experience that bordered on "frightening." I unpacked, took stock of my new surroundings and began to feel a depth of loneliness that would accompany me for the next five weeks.

Perhaps a few passages from my journal are the best way of sharing the pain, the richness of my desert/solitude experience.

"It was extremely difficult to pray the Morning Praise today. Each time I tried I thought of my sisters gathered in prayer as the community I love, and my eyes became so full that I could never read the words. I am sure that loneliness is an emotion keenly experienced in the desert, certainly it is mine. My heart however, is filled with gratitude and I know that my sisters are only as far as my heart allows them to be. Not far at all!"

"My prayer this morning was again tear-filled, not so much from missing my sisters as being touched by the Lord. As I breathed I LOVE YOU, I had the sense that Jesus was saying the same thing to me simultaneously so that it was just one prayer, not two. I believe that there has been a shift and that I may make it after all. I truly wondered, but begged for the grace."

"I awakened this morning to the most glorious sunrise spanning the sky with varied hues of rose and magenta. Who could ever doubt there is a God with such beauty as this spilling over the sleepy earth?"

"I am finding the days very long. It is like I have lost everyone and everything familiar — not unlike being lost in the desert. It is calling for such trust and surrender. I pray that I am able."

"Today has been a difficult day. Even very early this morning I couldn't pray. That excruciating feeling of loneliness swept over me and remained most of the day. I took Clare's letters to ponder and pray with as I poured out my heart. She pointed out a few facts to me in her motherly way. It was not just loneliness that I was experiencing but my own emptiness, my poverty which I was seeing as an enemy. Clare took my hand and led me down into that abyss of emptiness where Jesus was waiting. It was in my own heart. Clare said not only must I stay there, but that I must choose to go there. It is where I will find Jesus."

"The darkness has lifted and I feel the warmth of the sunlight enter my being. When I was walking up the hill today I found myself singing the first time since I have come here. This told me that I had moved to a different space. Clare has been very close to me and continues to help me keep my gaze on Jesus."

"As the days pass by I'm aware that the solitude is making me so vulnerable to suffering, not mine but that of others. I weep for our broken and torn world. I even ache for the dying plants and creatures that I see on my hikes. Much of my prayer time is spent with the suffering Christ and his broken body as I embrace all and take them into the heart of Christ where my heart has already been absorbed."

"Time here is winding down. Soon it will be time to leave. It will be so good to join my sisters again in community. How I have longed for that moment! But my time here has been blessed and rich. So I thank God, and my community, for this special time in prayer and solitude. Not all of it would I have chosen initially, but looking back I can see the wisdom of God's choice of opportunities that have opened me. I needed to experience such excruciating loneliness to learn that my heart was not totally given, that much of me was attached to the people whom I love and who love me. Not that that is wrong, but it does mean that all of me did not need God. I needed to experience it in order to let some surrender take place. My God has taught me through the isolated, wild desert that I needed to trust, that I needed to be tamed, that there is no place for fear. I feel so much more free, alive, purified, confirmed in love. I have discovered that "You are never less alone than when you are alone" (*The Hermitage Within*). It is now over a year since I have returned to the monastery and there is not a day when I do not recall my desert experience. Many times it is to remember a lesson learned in prayer, a relished desert sunset beyond describing, a memory of tears for someone in pain, a cherished touch of love. I have appreciated the gift of community in a way that I could never have thought possible. Truly, I believe that God emptied me so that He could fill me, and it still continues to be so.

Sister Doreen Trautman, O.S.C.
Duncan, B.C., Canada

"...this highest poverty has made you poor in the things of this world but exalted you in virtue." RCl 8:4b

Moving the Refrigerator at 67!

As one who has heard on more than one occasion, "You are helpless," it is not with a bit of amusement that at age 67 I am a bit of a Wonder Woman, helping to move a full-size refrigerator up two flights of stairs with the aid of two senior citizen nuns and our maintenance man.

Oddly enough, my attraction to a contemplative lifestyle did produce a listing of my abilities and supposed limitations, as I pondered the call to join Jesus in this adventure called Poor Clare living!

To my surprise I have held just about every job in the Monastery with the exception of one or two positions and this is a span of 45 years that I am considering. I even held the position of Maintenance which, a good deal of the time, consisted in calling the right handy man or repair shop.

I have an amusing memory, very precious one now, since my partner in the endeavor has moved on to the final goal of it all. Sister Marianne and I were sharing the maintenance job at one point in our long career. We had a new system installed on our huge furnace located in the basement. Sister didn't feel any more confident than I did about our maintenance assignment.

We had to turn on this new furnace apparatus to heat up the Monastery. It came with a very detailed plan. Push the green button and if such and such doesn't happen, proceed to the red button and listen for a certain sound. We carried out the plan and ran for all we were worth, expecting the explosion to be following after us. Of course when this did not happen, we laughed like school kids.

I realize that I belong to a church with a physically limited Pope for a leader who can summon scores of people, many of them young, to listen to whatever he has to say. This same church was turned on its axis by an elderly Pope who was elected to fill in for a couple of years. What a surprise Pope John 23rd turned out to be.

At 67 so much is still possible with God's help, and the adventure has not been boring.

Sister Elizabeth Mortell, O.S.C.
New Orleans, Louisiana

"Very frequently while Clare was prostrate on her face in prayer, she flooded the ground with tears and caressed it with kisses so that she might always seem to have her Jesus in her hands on whose feet her tears flowed and her kisses were impressed." LegCl 19:94

How God Changed My Life

I was born in a very small village on the southern tip of Jeju Island. Most of the people in the village were relatives of mine. They were almost all Buddhist combined with a folk religion. My mother was especially very fervent in this religion.

When I was in middle school, I first heard the word "church." Of course I had never seen one. In God's good providence, I was sent to a Catholic high school in Jeju City. Next to the school was a big church and some of our classes were given to us by priests and sisters. When we had a big event at school, all the students gathered for a Mass. The atmosphere at these Masses was very special. I also saw families attending church together and thought this was so beautiful that when I married I wanted to do the same with my family; however, I wasn't baptized until 10 years after my graduation. Although I had gone to Catechism classes, I tried to accept God only with my head and not in my heart. At this time my father died. This was my first experience of death. As he lay dying unable to speak or move, tears ran down his face. This was a great shock to me. I didn't know the meaning of these tears but I thought maybe he was afraid. This turned me completely around. I started searching for the Eternal. Before this my friends would sometimes take me to church but now I went on my own. I wanted to become a nun. I became very active in church and started reading spiritual books. My job as a teacher became second to my work in the church.

After my father died my family had many problems. The biggest was financial. My health became very poor and I had a very painful slipped disc in my back. I was getting ready to enter an active Franciscan Sisters' order but was asked to wait because of my bad health. When my family found out I wanted to become a Sister, they protested very strongly. I started wavering about my vocation. Now my world became to me like a prison. I could not find peace of heart no matter where I went. But sometimes I visited my friend, Sr. Julianna Kang at the Poor Clare Monastery. Little by little my heart was inclined to this Monastery. I started feeling I was called to the Poor Clare life.

With my family still opposed to my entering religious life and my health not completely recovered, I entered. The afternoon I entered I remember praying before the Blessed Sacrament and telling Jesus, "Here I am before you. At last I am yours." This prayer was very precious to me. After entering I finally found the true peace my heart sought.

I know how much God loves me, and God's love has always been with me through the love of my Sisters, my friends, and my family. God has lead me all my life. Now I can confess, "I love God." Without God, I cannot live.

My family are still as they were, fervent Buddhists, and they receive consolation from this. But I hope they will come to know God as I know God. I leave this in God's hands. My villagers are still just as they are too. Not one is a Christian yet. What a mystery that one from this village should be called to the contemplative life. I'm wondering what seeds my life will plant there for the future? I now want to share with them God's love.

Sister Theresa Oh, O.S.C.
Jeju Island, Korea

"This is the summit of the highest poverty which has established you, my dearest sisters, heiresses and queens of the kingdom of Heaven."   RC1 8:4a

Images and Dreams

I was born about the same time television became popular, yet it was a while before my family got one. I remember watching the story of St. Therese the Little Flower and crying myself to sleep that night. Images left very strong impressions on me, and Saint Therese was so pretty and her sad story caught me. (I came to know later in life that, being half-Scandinavian, the sadder side of life follows me like a shadow.) My father tried to console me by going to the store and buying me a new notebook for school. But the movie melded with my dreams and stayed with me. I knew that night I was going to be a nun, though I had no idea what that would mean.

In high school I asked to go to a convent boarding school, but my parents didn't like the idea. After high school I trained as a laboratory technician and worked for a couple of years. I then joined the postulancy of the Notre Dame School Sisters for nearly three years. Both they and I knew it was not a good match: I had not come up through the "aspirancy" (high school girls preparing for the convent). There was a clash because I had lived on my own for two years before joining. I left but couldn't let go.

At one point after my stay with the Notre Dame Sisters, I tried starting something with another "real" sister of Notre

Dame. We lived an "experiment," as it was called then, in the poor part of town. During that time we visited the local Poor Clare monastery in Minneapolis and all the feelings of my dream/movie vocation came back. I knew this was the place, but I didn't know how I would get there.

I returned to hospital work, joined the Peace Corps, and finished college by going part time. By now I was in my 30s and was regularly visiting the Monastery of St. Clare in Bloomington, Minnesota. I entered the monastery in the early 1980s. By the 1990s I felt this wasn't yet it.

Bishop Ken Untener invited four of us from Bloomington to move to Saginaw, Michigan. His invitation included a request to do something new. It was then that I knew I was at home to develop my vocation story. I took my final vows in Saginaw, and I have been here for 13 years.

Sister Laura Hammel, O.S.C.
Saginaw, Michigan

"As pilgrims and strangers in this world, serve the Lord in poverty and humility.."   *RCl 8*

Hiding in God's Dwelling Place

I grew up in a very fervent Protestant family, as my father was a minister, and my mother was an evangelist! When I was in about third grade, I suddenly started having seizures of an epileptic nature while I was sleeping during the night. My mother took me to hospitals, and I even took oriental medications for at least two years, but the doctors could find no medicine that helped me. Finally, as a last resort, when I was in fifth grade, mother took me to church at the dawn worship service, and the minister laid hands on me, praying for my healing. I was completely healed, and after that had no more seizures! To me this was so amazing, and I could hardly believe it. How could this happen through prayer? But, in fact, a miracle had happened!

From the time I was in middle school, I wanted to be a doctor, since I had experienced the suffering of this past illness. I shared much with my mother, just like I would a friend. Mother told me that I should never forget God's goodness to me, and always be thankful for the healing He had granted me. I really did feel so grateful, and wondered how I could express this thanks to God. As I gradually grew older, I thought that I wanted to be a person of God who could share God's goodness and love with others in some service to the poor, or to those in need. In thanksgiving for my own healing, I wanted to let people know how good God is!

I decided that I wanted to be a missionary! When I was in high school, my teacher said that I would make a good teacher, but my desire to be a missionary did not change. So, after graduation, with a joyful heart, I entered the Protestant seminary to prepare myself. It was in 1976, my fourth year of seminary college, that my friend, Martha Lee, whom I had known since high school, gave me two books to read. One of them was *Seven Storey Mountain* by Thomas Merton, and the other one was a book by Carlo Carretto. After reading these books I started to feel some interest in the Catholic Church, and in the contemplative life. Why in the world would very learned and intelligent people like these two men leave the world and live their whole lives in a contemplative monastery? I wanted to know more about contemplative monasteries, and since Martha was interested in the Jeju monastery, I decided to go there with her to visit.

Before this visit to Jeju, Martha asked me to attend Mass with her at the St. Lazarus Leper Village, where she was a volunteer. I really didn't want to do so, but because she asked me, I went. Of all the women in the Gospel, I liked Mary Magdalene the most and, later on, found out that this was the feast of St. Mary Magdalene. I was so deeply touched by all the prayers of the Mass! Each prayer expressing the history of our salvation was so beautiful and

special, as well as the intercession of the saints, the inter-
cessory prayers, the preface, etc. It was like falling in love
for me! I thought, "Ah, this is why Thomas Merton and
Carlo Carretto went into solitude!"

So, we went to Jeju for a visit to the monastery, and this
first visit was very peaceful, and not at all strange to me! We
met two of the sisters, and they radiated an interior beauty
and seemed full of life and so free! During the two days of
this visit, I shared many things with Sister Mary Frances, the
novice directress, asking questions about some of the
Catholic Church teachings. Even though I was from such
a strong Protestant background, it was amazing that I felt
no rejection of any of the Church's teachings! On the con-
trary, I already felt attracted to the Church, and wanted to
learn more. By the time I left the monastery, I had decided
in my heart that I wanted to be a contemplative sister - a
Poor Clare! I had no need or desire to find out about
another Order, or even another monastery. It was only Jeju
for me! This was October of 1979.

So, I studied the Catholic catechism for six months, and
in May of 1980 I was baptized. I hadn't told my family anything about this! I was so happy that I had to tell someone,
so I told one of my friends with whom I had gone to the
seminary. She went and told my mother, (my father had
already died before this), and a "war" started with my whole
family! I also told them that I wanted to be a contemplative

sister. No one could understand, and my whole family and relatives were terribly upset and felt disgraced by me. I was told that they would disown me! If I had wanted to be engaged in the active apostolate, perhaps I would not have had to convert to Catholicism, as active ministry was possible in the Protestant church, but I knew that I only had one body! Through prayer, more than any other activity, there were so many persons and places that I could reach.

Under these circumstances, I could no longer live at home, but I had to wait three years before I could enter the Jeju community. So I immigrated to the United States, where my brother lived. I needed distance from my mother, and she also needed time to deal with this situation that she could not accept or understand. While I was in the States, my mother and family kept checking to see if I still wanted to be a sister. Even though they couldn't understand, I couldn't let go of this deep desire and, after three years, there was no change in me. Although my brother felt sad, he came to a little understanding, and eventually my mother reluctantly agreed to let me go to Jeju, only for a three month's guest stay at the monastery, to "get it out of my system," and then come home and forget about it!

When I actually began to live in the monastery, there were many things in community life that I hadn't expected, and found difficult. However, my desire for God was so strong that I couldn't let go of that! Also, I would see the other sisters hanging on to their desires, and ask myself, "What is it that keeps them here?" All of them must also have had difficulties, but living in Christ was more important. The sisters and their love were a big strength and encouragement, which helped me to persevere to final vows.

Gradually, through prayer and God's gift, my mother's opposition changed, and at the time of my final vows, she received a great grace! Reading the liturgical profession ceremony ahead of time, she was deeply touched at its beauty, and decided that she, too, would offer herself to God anew, as I made my final commitment. That day was a very happy day for her, and she told our sisters that, more than being called an evangelist, now she is proud to call herself the mother of a sister, and mother of a minister. (My brother, in the meantime, had been ordained as a Protestant minister.)

Recently, I have come on a new Poor Clare foundation that our Jeju community has begun. As St. Clare gave herself in ardent love to the Lord, and lived the Gospel life in absolute poverty, choosing insecurity rather than a secure life, I, too, felt attracted to that kind of experience. I thought of St. Clare and how she lived at San Damiano. Whenever the mention of a new foundation came up in community, I experienced the desire for the adventure of this kind of a new beginning in simplicity and poverty. As Abraham left everything to follow God's Will, I feel called upon to rely on God's providence. Even though we have material insecurity now, I have faith in God. He will work everything out! I am sure of this, and this is my strength, my hope, my security and my joy!

Sister Clara (Hye Young) Park, O.S.C.
Yang Yang Community
(A new Poor Clare Foundation in Korea)

"Let the sisters be eager to preserve among themselves the unity of mutual love which is the bond of perfection."   RCl 10:7

Some Vocations
Do Not Come Overnight

It is always difficult to pinpoint the beginning of a vocation to serve God; the ending never comes, so it is no problem.

As a third grader in public school, daughter of Methodist parents, I fell head over heels in love with St. Francis of Assisi in the story in my reader of him preaching to the birds. That may not be the actual beginning, but it is one that I am willing to share. We moved to Mt. Rainier, Maryland, a suburb of Washington, D.C., and then moved into a smaller house across town, to find Catholics surrounded us except for one Jewish family. What we called the "valley" was like sand out of an hourglass cupped in the palm of your hand. Almost a visible boundary surrounded it.

Catherine, a neighbor girl living up the wooded hill and by the railroad track, invited me to my first Mass when I was ten. I did not understand any of it and, at the benediction of the Blessed Sacrament, I was certain that I would become a Catholic one day. With an anti-Catholic dad and siblings, Jesus would have to find a way to bring that about. He did.

At fifteen, we moved to Sullivan, Indiana. My parents did not want me to grow up in Maryland, marry and settle there so we pitched our tent on an old farm north of Sullivan, yet close enough to their people. The following year, Our Lady spoke to me from a stream of light one hot August day, about three months after World War II ended, saying, "You will one day go to Tokyo, Japan, and there you will become a Catholic."

I asked: "Okay, if you say so but how will you get me there?" Her response was: "You will join the army and go."...the furthest thing from my sixteen-year-old mind.

My mother died when I was twenty-one. The following year I was visiting my brother in California. He was re-called to Active Duty with the U.S. Navy and left me where I was.

This was where I sowed the hayseed in my hair, from farm life and my blissful ignorance of life to a port city in California. To protect people still living, let me say it was one o'clock in the morning. I was a bit angry at someone's conduct and was walking home past a concrete warehouse in the heart of the city. A Volkswagen full of young boys passed me, did a U-turn, then stopped. Four of them piled out and spread out so that I could not escape them. I put my hand on the rosary my Lutheran landlady had put around my neck for protection earlier in the evening and said a terrified prayer: "Lady of the Rosary, help me!" At that instant, the four outside the car stopped moving and spoke: "Look, she's not alone anymore. Where did She come from? Let's get out of here!" They scrambled back into the VW and took off with squealing tires like someone was after them. The voice I had heard on that country road in Indiana six years before spoke: "Do not be frightened. I will protect you." And in my side vision I could see her standing near, just above the sidewalk. Only then could I start to move. Mary talked as we walked home and said: "I want you to return to Indiana, straighten out your affairs and enter the Army. It is time to start your journey to Japan."

Only Lady Mary and I knew about that. I had never told it to anyone. I did as she said and on December 24, 1954, I entered the Church in Tokyo, Japan as she had said nine years before. She has not abandoned me in all these years since.

I resisted the vocation to the Poor Clares almost every step of the way. Step one I think was in a Ghost Town in Arizona near the Black Diamond Mine Ranch. A Franciscan Friar, in a small camper mobile home, was conducting a Mission there and the Fort Huachuca WAC Detachment was represented by three of us. Speaking to the friar afterward, on the last night of the Mission, I casually said: "Too bad there isn't an order like yours for women," and he directed me to the Poor Clares in Evansville, Indiana. I didn't get there for three years, meanwhile serving as a Secular Carmelite missionary in the military mission field.

I entered the Poor Clares but after two weeks I returned to the army. I went to Germany, trying to avoid what I sensed was God's assignment for me to France. The WAC Detachment was closed down four months later. I was sent to France. God does permit you to take detours, but gets you where He wants you in the end.

In Orleans, France, I taught catechism for the remainder of my tour of duty. And it was there that I began to write to Padre Pio of my spiritual struggles. In one letter, his English secretary wrote that Padre Pio was very interested in me and "that means he accepts you as his spiritual daughter." He has been a good spiritual director and got me to the Evansville Poor Clares and helped keep me here for 30 years.

As I like to tell people who are interested in our life, it is easy to enter and easy to leave, but darn hard to stay. You need all the spiritual assistance you can get. The struggle has been rewarding!

Sister Marie Carmel, O.S.C.
Evansville, Indiana

"Always observe the poverty and humility of our Lord Jesus Christ and of His most holy Mother and the Holy Gospel we have firmly promised."

RCl 12:13b

On the Learning Edge
The Firethrower

Growing up with a lively imagination and an energetic personality, I once perceived myself as a firethrower, one who takes the flame and boldly casts it forth.

It was in this stance that I decided to become a physician, dreaming about being a missionary in some far-off land, ministering to God's poor. Despite "the best laid plans..." someone stole my fire, or at least that's what it felt like to me.

It's not that the fire within me died, but that it was being pulled in another direction. I shared my inner struggle with my two best friends, a Religious Sister whom I greatly respected and my grandmother, who was my trusted "wisdom figure." In spite of some surprised responses and my own personal disbelief and anguish, it seemed that God was calling me to Religious life. However, getting to know the "real" firethrower would become my life project.

I did "catch" the flame and entered an apostolic religious order committed to education and nursing. My flame soared and shrank many times over 13 years and eventually I felt that I was being led in a different direction again. I was incredibly grateful for the opportunities for spiritual growth and enrichment, for professional education, for ministering to young people and for many wonderful friendships, some still enjoyed today. After much turmoil, prayer and consultation, I chose to trust the Spirit's promptings and left the congregation.

Sensing that I was leaping from the "frying pan into the fire," I buried myself in study, work and eventually, travel. My myopic, First World lifestyle was markedly challenged by traveling in the Middle East. Traumatic experiences in Israel shattered my "assumptive" world. My Israeli friend's cousin was stabbed outside the Old City in Jerusalem shortly before I arrived, my Palestinian friend's brother was shot on another corner while I was there, and my Christian friend told me that it was very dangerous to be seen with any of them! I'd never seen such extreme poverty as existed along the Nile River in Egypt. Even the destitute of Mexico seemed better off. Newspapers and TV portrayed a world perspective totally different from my comfortable image. This worldview often perceived the West as the "bad guys." How could this be? My values, both Christian and cultural, were thrown into confusion and questioning. I struggled with God to understand this upheaval that seared a path to the core of my beliefs. How could this God who so enflamed my own heart seem so manipulated by human ideologies and structures?

Returning home and to work, I immersed myself in the Peace Movement, augmenting action with study and reflection on the social message of the gospel. As a representative at the U.N. Special Session on Disarmament, I met many extraordinary people — humanitarians, those from various religions, and Christians deeply committed to working for justice and peace in our world, some willing to risk jail and others even death. My identity of what it meant to be a Christian was becoming more finely tuned.

Fueled by the courage of such dedicated people, I became part of one of the first justice and peace teams visiting Central America. Here I really "met" Jesus Christ. In the passionate struggle for human dignity, respect and freedom, the Spirit's call for God's reign to be present now on earth as in heaven was powerfully grasped by the poor and illiterate. Many Religious — Jesuits, Franciscans and others — assisted these ordinary people in that kind of prayerful reflection on the Gospels that captured the "both/and" of powerful devotion and Jesus' proclamation of the kingdom of God.

Plunged into the depths of human compassion and mercy on the one hand and witnessing the gross inhumanity and cruelty of Western-taught tactics of war on the other, my vocation to the Poor Clares lay smoldering. After having prayed together, our team visited a small barrio. I raised the question: "How can we best help you?" Some said they needed money to rebuild bombed health clinics and schools, some said more peacemakers should come, others suggested changing Western government policies toward developing countries and several cried, "Please pray."

Once again, I felt pulled in several directions, all ways of more conscious discipleship, but the deepest question was "How was God calling me?" What flame would God ignite in me, now?

Those people who lived on the learning edge of life echoed what Jesus of Nazareth, Francis and Clare of Assisi and countless others grasped. It is contemplation, gazing on the face of Christ and letting him gaze back on you, not weapons or power of any sort, that transforms hearts. It is in response to this kind of suffering love that impels us to forge paths of surrender to Christ so that we can be Christ for others.

As I prayed, read, and sought wisdom from good friends, the spirits of Francis and Clare kept beckoning me, stretching me to embrace the Poor Christ as they did. After reading St. Clare's Legend, the Process of Canonization, and Clare's own writings I was deeply moved by her profound personal relationship with God and the immense challenges she confronted so tenaciously. Immediately I sensed that if Clare's sisters imbibed her spirit they would be acutely aware of the needs and aspirations of others. And this group of women did not disappoint me!

Even though I was middle aged, a competent professional, with previous experience in religious life, nothing could prepare me for the interior surrender necessary to follow the Gospel Project of Clare and Francis.

The Firethrower was now casting a fire that completely consumed me. The rhythm of prayer, work, study, leisure and community living keeps one focused on the one thing necessary: to "totally respond to Christ's love who totally gave himself up for our love."

I have come full circle. I recognize that within the ebb and flow of our human condition a flame will soar and wane. But it is in the fiery furnace of Love where it blazes, burning away the excessive focus on self. This is the heart of the Franciscan Contemplative — to become prayer, to enter into the intimate exchange of Love and allow the only Firethrower to set the world ablaze!

Sister Joyce Harris, O.S.C.
Duncan, B.C., Canada

"By most perfect poverty she (Clare) was eager to conform to the Poor Crucified..."

LegCl 14

God's Ways Are Mysterious!

Who would think that I would be able to become a Poor Clare after being turned down five times by other orders due to my age of fifty-five years?

My mentor, a contemplative sister of the Good Shepherd, advised me to write to the Poor Clares in Omaha. Within two weeks, I received a letter saying that I could "come and see" what the Lord's Will would be. With St. Francis, I could say, "This is what I wish, this is what I seek, this is what I long to do with all my heart": To follow the poor Christ.

The children were not surprised when I told them that I was going to Omaha to enter the monastery. I had told them after their father died that God was calling me to give my life totally to Him.

They responded to this grace by being very open to God's Will for me. When I arrived at the monastery, the Lord held me as a lamb in His arms, placed me down and said, "Stay and never go out there again." This confirmed my desire to become a Poor Clare.

Sister Clarissa Leyendecker, O.S.C.
Omaha, Nebraska

"Clare was vigilant in prayer and sublime contemplation."   Proc 6:3

Called to Love

As I reflect on my life, I see only many graces. The first thing that comes to my mind is how all things came to me through love.

I was born the youngest of seven children in a very strict Confucian family. My father accepted the position of superintendent at a Catholic high school when I was three years old. Because of this we all became Catholic, including my grandparents. After this I spent most of my time at church. I went to Sunday school and was active in Catholic clubs. From my youngest years until in my 20s, I practically lived at Church. I was also a Sunday school teacher. From the age of 16, I started thinking of a religious vocation. My mother died suddenly. I went to see our parish Sister, as she always accepted me and consoled me no matter when I went there. Later I learned she did this with each and every one in our parish. She brought us close to God. I realized how much one person could do in loving like this. I was very impressed and wanted to be like her. This is exactly what our world needed, I thought.

Some years passed. I was working at the Seo-Jong Culture Center very close to the Franciscan Friars. In my spare time, I would visit and pray in their chapel. I became a life-long friend with many of the priests.

When they had some special ceremony they would invite me. Because of this I was able to see them at work and at prayer in a natural setting. They lived together in a Friary without much external comfort, but they were always joyful. My older sister, too, had joined a secular institute and she lived very poorly but always was happy. This made me wonder what their secret was and, as I questioned this in my heart, I started changing. I started reading the Bible and spiritual books. Martin Buber's books especially helped me. I could feel God leading me. I went to a Franciscan priest for the sacraments and for spiritual guidance. He introduced me to the Jeju Poor Clares.

When my vacation time came, I made a retreat at the Monastery. This was my first retreat, and it seemed such a long way from Seoul. During my retreat we celebrated a beautiful Feast of St. Clare. After returning to Seoul, the Sisters remained with me. My whole being was still in the Monastery. The sisters seemed very poor but rich in freedom and joy. How did this come about? Another mystery for me! The question I kept asking myself was: "Did they fall in love with Jesus and choose to live enclosure?" One day I fell in love with Jesus and wanted to give my all. I entered the Monastery loving the Resurrected Jesus. The Crucified Jesus at this time was hard for me to understand. Jesus dying on the cross was too idealistic, I thought. But as I lived this life following in the spirit of Francis and Clare and receiving love from the Sisters, I started loving the

Crucified Christ also. All my weaknesses, limitations and sufferings were tools to bring me to be one with Jesus and His love. I also experienced great joy and freedom in this life. In my prayer I felt the poor and suffering of this world were absorbed into the mercy and love of God, and I was one with them and with God. My calling here fulfilled my longing to become love for others. The enclosure and our silent life, my sinfulness and my weakness, these all became tools for me to receive even more graces.

Through the Word of God I know God has been leading me. In 1997 during my sojourn in Brenham, Texas, with our Sisters there, I felt God leading me to the desert like the prophet Hosea says and speaking to my heart. I was greatly consoled. After I came back to Korea, I had some health problems, but the Word of God I kept hearing in my mind was, "God is Love." Soon after this I found out I had colon cancer and needed surgery. Strange as it may sound, my stay in the hospital was the most blessed time in my whole life so far. My whole life was in God's hands, and I was in great peace. At my side was a loving Sister to help me recover. I felt so loved. At my retreat two years later, while staying with our Sisters in Duncan, the Word of God was from John 21:18-19. I knew I had to let God lead me, and I had to accept being lead wherever that was. I have been blessed to be able to share with many Sisters in the various Monasteries. Each one has helped deepen my vocation and made me richer in joy and grace. Also always in my heart are our dear Sisters Frances and Marianne. With St. Clare I can say, "Truly I can rejoice and no one can rob me of such joy since at last what under heaven I desired I have received." (Third letter to Agnes) I simply want to say, "thank you so much."

Sister Cecilia Pak, O.S.C.
Jeju Island, Korea

"...have humility and patience in difficulty and infirmity."   RCl 10:10b

My Second Mother and My Friend

The third child in a family of five, I was about nine years old when my mother died and I depended a lot on my two older sisters for support and guidance. One became the "mother" and the one who was next to me in age became "my friend." We talked about many things, one of which was my desire to be a nun when I grew up. We shared hours together making plans about what we would do with our lives. Because of circumstances, Dad was not able to keep us together as a family, and we were placed in foster homes.

When I was twelve years old, I went to the home of the Karwoski family; there I began to adjust my life anew, in a loving, caring, and happy family. I stayed with this family during the rest of my teenage years. Julia Karwoski was like a mother to me. She taught me how to cook and bake and was very watchful about my dating. Christmas and Easter were very special times around the Karwoski household. Mom Karwoski would cook her delicious Polish omelet and great Italian chili. The laughter was abundant as the family gathered to decorate the Christmas tree and put the nativity scene in its special place. Mom Karwoski filled those teen years with lots of love, protection and guidance. I am sure that it was here that my desire to enter Religious life began in earnest!

Sister Jane Louise Wade, O.S.C.
Spokane, Washington

"Have compassion for the afflicted."   *Proc 3:3*

New Life Through Death

Through my father's death I was reborn. He died when I was 21 years old. A year later my mother died. I was very close to my father. He was not only a dad to me but also a close friend.

We were not a Catholic family; however, my father wanted to be baptized on his deathbed. Because he now was a "Catholic," after he died the parish members came to our house and prayed the prayers for the dead. The leader among them told me if I wanted my father to go to heaven, I had to also pray these prayers often. Of course I wanted my beloved father to go to heaven and I wanted to help him in any way I could, so I prayed and I prayed not knowing what I was saying. I didn't understand one bit what the prayers meant. In order to understand what I was praying, I decided to become a Catholic. I felt this would help my father even more. Even after studying the catechism and becoming baptized, I really didn't understand my new faith. Then on Sunday going to Mass, I saw an advertisement for a Catholic catechetical school. I applied to attend this school to learn more about my faith.

In attending this school, I was able to see a lot of Sisters. I looked around and discovered how they lived. I thought their lives must be very difficult. I didn't have any confidence that I could live that life but I remember once before my father died some friends and I were talking about what we wanted to become in the future. I don't know why I said what I did, but I suddenly said without knowing even the meaning of the words, "I want to become a nun."

I was the youngest of nine children. I was raised with a lot of freedom, attention, and protection from hardships. After my parents died my older sisters took me under their wings. They wanted for me what they themselves could never have had. They also expected great things from me. While at the catechetical school I decided to become a Sister.

After I graduated, I decided I had to live alone and away from my sisters. I chose the farthest and the most difficult place I could find so I could experience hardship. I found the Isidore Ranch on Jeju Island. I went there in 1976. I worked very hard among the farmers, many times not getting to bed until 2 or 3 in the morning. I attended daily Mass at the Poor Clare Monastery next to the Isidore Farm. After Mass, I would stay and pray for another 30 minutes or more in private. At this time I was very tired and exhausted but one day, listening to the Gospel, I found a new life stirring in me. The gospel was of Mary and Martha serving Jesus. This struck me as never before. I had always been like Martha, but all of a sudden I wanted to be like Mary, sitting at the feet of Jesus. This Monastery was where I wanted to be.

A few days later I heard Sr. Frances Kwon say, "Wouldn't it be nice if one or two would enter now that we have a new Novitiate?" When I heard that, I knew I had to knock at the Monastery door and ask to enter.

God was preparing my vocation from the time of my father's death. I've had many trials, but in each one I found the grace to live more deeply my vocation. My faith has become stronger and stronger. Without this faith I could not have survived.

Another big blessing for me came on the first Sunday of Advent in 2001. Before this, my father was the big influence in my life but on this Sunday with our Blessed Mother saying her "fiat," I saw my own mother and wanted to become more motherly, too. I had neglected the mother side of myself but on that Sunday, I was inspired by my own mother and our Blessed Mother to become like them saying "fiat" to all in life. I have become much more gentle because of this grace and know a fullness of joy and peace.

Sister Theresa Cho, O.S.C.
Jeju Island, Korea

"...pray always to Him with a pure heart."   *RCl 10:10A*

A Question Of Divine Providence

Time is one of the greatest mysteries in human life. It should be simply a matter of ticks on an old-fashioned clock or the steady passing of seconds on a modern digital face variety. Like music, time speeds up and slows down according to the beating of the human heart. Forty-one years can be a long, long time or it can be but a breath. When I am asked how long I have been in the Monastery, I respond, "Forty-one years!" and yet in my mind I can still be the child in this story, which really happened some fifty years ago.

In the parochial school system in Louisiana in the 1950s it was the custom that the sacrament of Confirmation was received by students in the sixth grade. In the lower grades a student would hear rumors from the "upper class" about the mysteries surrounding the reception of the Sacrament which included a day of retreat — whatever that might be. When I reached the sixth grade, our Sister engaged us in a competition of correct answers from the catechism as part of our preparation for Confirmation. I no longer remember the "prize" to be won, only the contest itself. By the month of October there were only two girls in the class who had not missed the correct response to a catechism question when called upon. I was proud to be one of those two. One day I came home from school and did not feel like studying that weekend. So instead of tackling my memorization I just had fun. What I did I cannot remember, but I am sure it must have been worth the risk of losing my prestigious position. That Monday morning I woke up in "terror" realizing that all my prestige might be lost. So I opened my green Catechism and tried to cram. I only had time to absorb one question and answer:

"What is Divine Providence?

Divine Providence is God's loving care for us."

I held my breath when it came time for Catechism class. I slipped down into my desk so as not to be conspicuous. Then came the moment of truth and Sister read out the question: "What is Divine Providence?" and looked around for someone to call upon. Her gaze fell on me and I was able to supply the answer to the question. That day my status and prestige were saved but more importantly that day I was given the key to the answer of life and its meaning and mystery.

Shortly after this amazing moment my family left the city of New Orleans and we moved to Memphis, Tennessee. I missed receiving the sacrament of Confirmation with my class and came to a Church where this sacrament was bestowed on first or third graders according to the rotation cycle of the bishop who lived far away in Nashville. I was in the eighth grade before it was possible to receive the sacrament.

During my junior year our parish acted as a host to a city-wide Vocation Day. Because I lived so close to the Church I decided that I might as well go and see what might be there. It was a day with very few young people attending. It was hard to be inconspicuous as the little group of classmates I was mingling with went from booth to booth. I came to the table with literature on the Poor Clares and Sr. Mary Angela, a Poor Clare extern sister, asked me, "Do you think there will be more young people attending?" I replied "Sister, I have never been to anything like this before. I really don't know!" Years later I would remind her of our encounter. There might have been few girls present, but they did receive a vocation in the end.

I kept the literature from all the various communities in the bottom drawer of my dresser. I left the Vocation Day strongly drawn to the Good Shepherd Sisters. I especially liked the large silver heart that they wore as part of their habit. The idea of working with troubled teenagers was appealing. Only during the senior retreat did it seem clear to me that I was being asked by our Lord to go to the Monastery of St. Clare. It seemed a strange choice to me as it appeared that a cloistered life would be a life of introspection and self concern — inclinations I already had abundantly and did not think it would be too healthy to foster. I prayed — I will go and try this way of life to show You, Lord, that it is not for me. After forty-one years I have to admit I believe that the Spirit did know what form of religious life would fit me best and would enable me to blossom into the kind of person He knew I could become. This form of life fashioned by St. Clare is the embodiment of living each day in response to the mystery of Divine Providence.

To be a Poor Clare is to live in a constant surrender to the mystery of Divine Providence. The struggle to maintain a real form of poverty is not to be poor for the sake of being poor. It is a form of life, which daily says — God will provide whatever we need whenever we need it, and we do not have to live in fear that He will not. Our Monastery is rich in stories of how God spoils us by providing not only our needs but even our smallest wishes. In the early days our Monastery was heated with a coal furnace, but one day the coal bin was empty. The Abbess called the community together and they began to pray that the Lord would send them help. As they were praying in the chapel, they heard a voice calling from the extern church: "Coal! Coal!" One of the sisters went outside and found a man with a truckload of coal! Another time the community was receiving their founding Abbess from Indiana for a visit. She had a very delicate stomach and the sisters in Memphis were anxious to have something she could eat. Hours before the Abbess arrived, a benefactor came to the door with some graham crackers, which was actually the food item they were hoping to have for her. In our own days we find that this sweet and loving care of our God for us also extends to the other poor folk who come to our door for help. Often we get items that we really do not need but have on hand because a poor person is coming with exactly that need. It is a joy to be an emissary of the Lord's providence as well as to be the recipient of this blessing.

We live in a world that prizes control and self-reliance. As St. Clare's daughters we witness to the true human condition that we have no control and must depend on God and on each other in order to be fully alive. Ours is a daring form of life in light of our culture, which always seeks what is secure. We awake every morning not knowing what the day will bring, but certain that God's loving care will surround us and in our poverty give us new reasons to praise His name.

Sister Mary Helen Kelley, O.S.C.
Memphis, Tennessee

The most holy virgin...silently addressed her soul and was heard to say: "Go without anxiety for you have a good escort for your journey. Go for He who created you has made you holy. And, always protecting you as a mother her child, He has loved you with a tender love. May You be blessed, O Lord, You Who have created my soul!" When one of the sisters asked her to whom she was speaking, Clare replied: "I am speaking to my blessed soul." Turning to another daughter, she said: "Do you see, O child, the King of glory Whom I see?"

LegCl 46

The Evangelical Life of Saint Clare

"His Grace is sufficient for me" 2 Corinthians 13: 9

In the early years of Clare's life, wars occurred between factions aligned with the Emperor and those loyal to the Pope. When the Communards defeated the nobles of Assisi, Clare and her family went into exile in Perugia. She saw famine in her land when crops failed on at least two occasions. After she began life at San Damiano the political and social upheavals continued.

Clare writes in her Rule: "When the Blessed Father saw that we had no fear of poverty, hard work, suffering, shame or contempt from the world ... he wrote for us a form of life...." Clare's was not a retiring life of comfort and security. During the first sixteen years at San Damiano, she worked as a servant among her sisters and was always available to people who came with their needs. After Clare became ill she offered another form of service: fidelity to the gospel in physical weakness and suffering. The *Legend of Clare*, compiled for her canonization in 1255, states that Clare learned the *Office of the Cross*, arranged by Francis for his daily prayer. Here she found communion with her Lord and the strength to carry on through twenty-nine years of illness. She was taken from her sick bed on two occasions to pray and bolster the courage of her sisters in the face of marauding soldiers.

In 1252, nearing the end of her life, Clare shaped her Rule. She took passages from the Franciscan rules, and from usages tested by time and the experience of the sisters at San Damiano. She seamed these together with her own peerless wisdom. Clare audaciously asked and eventually received papal approval of her rule as she lay dying. This *Rule of Clare* is a great legacy that Clare has left the human family, and particularly her daughters.

The *Testament of Clare* most likely was composed at a later date. Great similarity exists between the *Rule of Clare* and the *Testament*, with large passages lifted one from the other. Due to the scarcity of a manuscript tradition, some specialists doubted the authenticity of the *Testament* as a work of Clare. The recovery of a 14th century manuscript in the Poor Clare Monastery of Montevergine in Messina, Italy, bolstered the argument for authenticity. Most recently a specialist in the study of manuscripts has published the theory that the Messina manuscript might well be dated from the 13th century and have come from the hand of Brother Leo, an early companion of Francis and lifelong friend to Clare. If anyone knew the mind of Clare, it was Leo. The Testament begins with gratitude to the "Father of Mercies" for all that Clare has received, but most especially for "our vocation." The writing continues in an autobiographical fashion, sharing Clare's vocation story from the earliest awakening until her final prayer for perseverance.

"For this reason I bend my knee to the Father of our Lord Jesus Christ that, through the supporting merits of the glorious and holy Virgin Mary, His Mother, and of our most blessed father Francis and all the saints, the Lord Himself, who has given a good beginning, will also give the increase and final perseverance." *Testament*

The women who come to Clarian life today come from a social milieu quite different from that of Clare and the early Franciscans. The early Franciscans met the challenges to gospel life in their culture and epoch. Our moment in time is different with its unique challenges and opportunities. Poor Clares of today know that God who has given us a good beginning will be faithful to the end.

Sister Beth Lynn, O.S.C.
Minneapolis, Minnesota

The Blessing of Saint Clare

May the Lord bless you and keep you. May He show His face to you and be merciful to you. May He turn His countenance to you, my sisters and daughters, and give peace to you and to all others who come and remain in your company as well as to others now and in the future, who have persevered in every other monastery of the Poor Ladies.

I, Clare, a servant of Christ, a little plant of our most holy Father Francis, a sister and mother of you and the other poor sisters, although unworthy, beg our Lord Jesus Christ through His mercy and the intercession of His most holy Mother Mary and blessed Michael the Archangel and all the holy angels of God, of our blessed father Francis and all men and women saints, that the heavenly Father give you and confirm for you this most holy blessing in heaven and on earth. On earth may He multiply you in His grace and His virtues among His servants and handmaids in His Church Militant. In heaven, may He exalt you and glorify you among his men and women saints in His Church Triumphant.

I bless you during my life and after my death, as I am able, out of all the blessings with which the Father of mercies has and does bless His sons and daughters in heaven and on earth and a spiritual father and mother have blessed and bless their spiritual sons and daughters. Amen.

Always be lovers of your souls and those of all your sisters. And may you always be eager to observe what you have promised the Lord.

May the Lord always be with you and may you always be with Him. Amen. (Blessing of 1253)

Wrapped in Joy

Acknowledgments

A very special thank you to each of my Poor Clare Sisters for sharing your stories. Because of your courage and trust, we have this incredible book to share with the world!

Sincerest thanks and deepest gratitude to Debra Hampton who has been a godsend in my life, believing in *Wrapped in Joy* from the very beginning, and all that you have put into this book to help it become the masterpiece that it is. We all appreciate your total commitment to our Vocation project.

Our deepest gratitude to:

Fr. Murray Bodo, O.F.M., for the Welcome; Sr. Frances Teresa, O.S.C., for the Introduction; and Sr. Beth Lynn, O.S.C., for the Preface and inspired writings on the Evangelical Life of St. Clare;

Fr. Regis J. Armstrong, O.F.M., CAP, for permission to use the quotes from his book, *Clare of Assisi, Early Documents*, 1988 edition;

For all in our Franciscan Family along with our Franciscan Friars at the Development Offices and to all the newspaper and magazine book review editors who encouraged me and gave me much needed information;

Sister Clare Ellen Wittman, O.S.C., for her original watercolor of Clare on our cover and also for Sister's "Clare at San Damiano" (p. 238 Part 6).

Poor Clare Colettine Sisters in Cleveland; to Mother Jude, P.C.C., Sister Mary St. Paul, P.C.C., and Sister Mary Veronica, P.C.C., for allowing me to use the artwork from a 13th c. Drawing "Francis Receiving Clare" taken from their book *Clothed With Gladness* (p. 27).

Mark Balma for permission to use his original buon fresco on panel of St. Clare, *Clare: A New Guide to Women, Peace and Prayer*, commissioned by the Frescoes for Assisi Foundation for the 800th Anniversary of Saint Clare 1993. Exhibited in the Basilica of Santa Chiara October 1993 through March 1994. Now on display in the Museum of Sacred Art, San Rufino, Assisi, Italy (p. 83).

Father Emery Tang, O.F.M., for use of his snapshot taken of the Poor Clares at the Santa Barbara Mission in California in 2001 (p. 129).

Friar Vincent Petersen, O.F.M., Conv. for a first-time showing of his original painting, "Clare in the Garden" as presented to our Poor Clare Sisters in Minneapolis. To Sister Caroline Berres, O.S.C., for her photographic help (p. 203).

Sr. Marie Céline, O.S.C., and our Mission, B.C., Canada Sisters for permission to use the Icon of Clare, painted by Brother Claude Lane, O.S.B. (p. 245).

A Very Special Thank You To:

Sr. Doris Gerke, O.S.C., for believing in me and encouraging me to "take the ball and run with it;" to Sister Dianne Doughty, O.S.C., and Sr. Charlene Toups, O.S.C., for their loving support and help; and Sister Patricia Proctor, O.S.C.;

Sister Gabriel, O.S.C., who has stood by me and encouraged me; for your commitment to me and *Wrapped in Joy*, for sharing in my joy and supporting me.

My sister, Michelle Quinn, always there for me when there was a question of "Proper English"…for all your excellent suggestions and help and incredible patience!

Our Sisters Diane Ackerman, O.S.C., and Madonna Winkels, O.S.C., for translating their Sisters' stories from Korean to English; and to all other Poor Clares who assisted their Sisters so their stories could be included here and enjoyed by all;

The staff of Office Systems Center; Ray Alstrom; and Norris C. Broussard for their computer help;

Barbara Wilcox, Colleen Acerra, Theresa Dent, and Dr. Nancy Hilbert, Stephanie Spears, Connie Trevino, Ann Acerra, Sharon Rangnow, Liz Jaschke and Beverly Tuttle for their generous help in keeping community work flowing while I was "buried" in this marvelous book;

Sister Evelyn, IWBS, and her community, especially Sr. Frances Cabrini and Sr. Clementine;

All the priests, religious and laypeople who have been keeping us all wrapped in prayer.

What a wonderful support system you have been for us. For each of you, I ask for an outpouring of God's abundant blessings.

Additional Readings on Saint Clare

Clare of Assisi, Early Documents, revised and expanded, Regis J. Armstrong, O.F.M., Cap., Franciscan Institute Publications, St. Bonaventure University, 1993

Clare of Assisi, Marco Bartoli, trans. Sister Frances Teresa, O.S.C., Franciscan Press, Quincy University, 1993

Francis and Clare, The Complete Works, ed. and trans. Regis J. Armstrong, O.F.M., Cap., and Ignatius C. Brady, O.F.M., Paulist Press, 1982 (www.paulistpress.com)

Living the Incarnation, Praying with Francis and Clare of Assisi, Sister Frances Teresa, O.S.C., Franciscan Press, 1996

This Living Mirror, Reflections on Clare of Assisi, Sister Frances Teresa, O.S.C., Orbis Books, 1995

Clare, A Light in the Garden, Murray Bodo, O.F.M., St. Anthony Messenger Press, 1992

To Cling With All Her Heart to Him, The Spirituality of St. Clare of Assisi, Benet A. Fonck, O.F.M., Franciscan Press, 1996

Clare Among Her Sisters, Rene-Charles Dhont, O.F.M., The Franciscan Institute of St. Bonaventure University, 1987

Wrapped in Joy

A Retreat with Francis and Clare of Assisi, Following Our Pilgrim Hearts, Murray Bodo, O.F.M., and Susan Saint Sing, St. Anthony Messenger Press, 1996

Clare of Assisi: A Biographical Study, Ingrid J. Peterson, O.S.F., Franciscan Press, Quincy University, 1993

Clare and Her Sisters, Lovers of the Poor Christ, Madaline Pecora Nugent, S.F.O., Daughters of St. Paul, Boston, Massachusetts, 2003

Clare of Assisi...Friend of Francis, Bride of Christ, Rita M. Hickey, O.S.C., St. Clare Monastery, New Orleans, Louisiana, 1987

Monastery Directory

(www.poorclare.com)

The stories in this book come from Poor Clare Sisters in the Mother Bentivoglio and Holy Name Federations. Their addresses (and other Poor Clare locations) are as follows:

Mother Bentivoglio Federation:

St. Clare Monastery, 170 St. Paul Street, R.R. 1, Alexandria, Ontario, Canada K0C 1A0

Monastery of St. Clare, 9300 Highway 105, Brenham, TX 77833

Sancta Clara Monastery, 4200 No. Market Ave., Canton, OH 44714-1295

Monastery of St. Clare, 1505 Miles Road, Cincinnati, OH 45231-2427

St. Clare Monastery, 2359 Calais Road, Duncan, B.C. Canada V9L 5V5

Monastery of the Poor Clares, 6825 Nurrenbern Road, Evansville, IN 47712-8518

Monastery of St. Clare, 1310 Dellwood Avenue, Memphis, TN 38127-6399

Monastery of St. Clare, 8650 Russell Ave., Minneapolis, MN 55431-1998

St. Clare Monastery, P.O. Box 3370, Mission, B.C., Canada V2V 4J5

Monastery of St. Clare, 720 Henry Clay Ave., New Orleans, LA 70118-5891

Byzantine Nuns of St. Clare, 6688 Cady Rd., North Royalton, OH 44133-6399

Monastery of St. Clare, 3626 No. 65th Ave., Omaha, NE 68104-3299

Sisters of St. Clare, 4875 Shattuck Rd., Saginaw, MI 48603-2962

Monastery of St. Clare, 4419 No. Hawthorne St., Spokane, WA 99205-1399

Monastery of St. Clare, 107 No. Depot St., Victoria, TX 77901-6826

Sisters of St. Clare, Buk Gun Hallim Eup Kum Ak Ri, Jeju Island, So. Korea 695-830

St. Clare's Monastery, Kangwondo, Sokcho Shi, No Hak Dong 741-48, 43/3, So. Korea 217-070

Madres Clarisas, Corral Chiquito, Apartado 12, Huehuetenango, Guatemala 13901

Holy Name Federation:

Monastery of St. Clare, 445 River Road, Andover, MA 01810-4213

Monastery of St. Clare, 150 White Pine Rd., Chesterfield Township, Columbus, NJ 08022

Christ the King Monastery of St. Clare, 3900 Sherwood Blvd., Delray Beach, FL 33445-5699

San Damiano Monastery of St. Clare, 6029 Estero Blvd., Ft. Myers Beach, FL 33931-4325

Monastery of St. Clare, 416 2nd Ave. S.W., Great Falls, MT 59404-2904

Monastery of St. Clare, 1916 No. Pleasantburgh Dr., Greenville, SC 29609-4090

Monastery of St. Clare, 920 Centre St., Jamaica Plain, Boston, MA 02130-3099

Monastery of St. Clare, 1271 Langhorne-Newtown Rd., Langhorne, PA 19047-1297

Monastery of St. Clare, 86 Mayflower Ave., New Rochelle, NY 10801-1615

Wrapped in Joy

Other Poor Clare Locations:

Mary, Mother of the Church Monastery, 2505 Stonehedge Dr., Alexandria, VA 22306-2451

Monastery of the Blessed Sacrament, 4201 NE 18 Avenue, Amarillo, TX 79107-4201

St. Joseph Monastery of Poor Clares, P. O. Box 160, 1671 Pleasant Valley Rd., Aptos, CA 95001-0160

Poor Clare Monastery of Our Lady of Mercy, 300 North 60th St., Belleville, IL 62223-3927

Monastery of the Holy Ghost, 1820 Edwards Road, Bendigo, Vic. 3550, Australia

Our Lady of the Angels Monastery, 5817 Old Leeds Rd., Birmingham, AL 35210-2198

Monastery of Immaculate Conception, 6119 S. Austin Ave., Chicago, IL 60638

Monastery of the Blessed Sacrament, 3501 Rocky River Dr., Cleveland, OH 44111-2998

Adoration Monastery, 4108 Euclid Ave., Cleveland, OH 44103-3728

Our Lady of Light Monastery, 3325 Pecos St., Denver, CO 80211-3520

Maria Regina Mater Monastery, 1175 N. County Road, 300W, Kokomo, IN 46901

Poor Clare Monastery of the Immaculate Conception, 12210 S. Will Cook Rd., Lemont, IL 60439

Monastere Ste. Clare, 313 Rue Queen, Lennoxville, Sherbrooke, Quebec, Canada J1H 5J7

Immaculate Heart Monastery of Poor Clares, 28210 Natoma Rd., Los Altos, CA 94022-3299

Annunciation Monastery of Poor Clares, 6200 E. Minooka Rd., Minooka, IL 60447-9458

Monastery of Poor Clares, 28 Harpersville Road, Newport News, VA 23601-2322

Our Land of Angels Convent, 3432 W. Baskin Ridge, Peoria, IL 61604-1710

St. Joseph Monastery, 2311 Stockham Lane, Portsmouth, OH 45662-3049

Monastere Ste. Clare, 7 Rue Pelletier, Riviere-du-Loup, Quebec, Canada, G5R 1E7

Corpus Christi Monastery, 2111 South Main St., Rockford, IL 61102-3591

Monastery of Our Lady of Guadalupe, 809 E. 19th St., Roswell, NM 88201-7599

Monastery of St. Clare of the Immaculate Conception, 200 Marycrest Dr., St. Louis, MO 63129-4813

Monastery of Poor Clares, 215 East Los Olivos St., Santa Barbara, CA 93105-

St. Clare's Monastery, 421 South 4th St., Sauk Rapids, MN 56379-1898

Monastere Ste. Clare, 1200 Chemin Des Petriotes, Sorel, Quebec, Canada, J3P 2M7

Monastere Ste. Claire de L'Immaculee Conception, 55 Rue Ste. Claire, Valleyfield, Quebec, Canada, J6S 1N5

Poor Clares of Perpetual Adoration, 3900 13th St., N.E., Washington, D.C. 20017-2699

Monastery of St. Veronica Giuliani, 816 Jefferson St., Wilmington, DE 19801-1432

Wrapped in Joy

Abbreviations

1LAg	*The First Letter to Blessed Agnes of Prague*
2LAg	*The Second Letter of Blessed Agnes of Prague*
3LAg	*The Third Letter of Blessed Agnes of Prague*
4LAg	*The Fourth Letter of Blessed Agnes of Prague*
LEr	*The Letter to Ermentrude of Bruges*
RCl	*The Rule of Saint Clare*
TestCl	*The Testament of Saint Clare*
BCl	*The Blessing of Saint Clare*
LAgA	*The Letter of Saint Agnes of Assisi*
Not	*The Notification of the Death of Saint Clare*
Proc	*The Acts of the Process of Canonization*
LegCl	*The Legend of Saint Clare*
CantExh	*The Canticle of Exhortation of St. Francis*

All the quotes used after the Sisters' stories have been taken, with permission, from *Clare of Assisi – The Early Documents,* as edited and translated by Regis J. Armstrong, O.F.M., Cap., 1988 edition.

About Sister Katherine, O.S.C.

I've written my spiritual journey which can be found on page 58. The publisher requested I tell you more about me. In all the books I've read, people use this section to tell everyone about their accomplishments in life; their many degrees and honors; the books they've written; the many workshops they've conducted. I don't have any great accomplishments so to speak. However, I have been blessed by God in His allowing me to compile the Sisters' stories for *Wrapped in Joy*. I am truly blessed!

I have lived a good life as full of joy and gladness as I could make it. The one thing I have done in abundance is: I have loved much … and I have laughed a lot … hopefully spread lots of joy … and that ability I know is a great grace from God for which I am eternally grateful!

I never knew I had anything in common with our blessed Father Francis until, in studying his life, I read that he loved a good time, enjoyed having a crazy time with his friends and how he turned all that energy into loving and following our Lord Jesus. It's nice to know that I was in such good company.

Having been born and brought up in Brooklyn, New York, I was educated by the School Sisters of Notre Dame and attended St. Saviour High School. Upon graduation, I attended The Wood School and got a great preparation for entering the business world. I spent many wonderful years with, among others, IBM. I never stayed too long in any one area. I'd learn the work and travel on to learn more. I've had great opportunities presented to me; I've made wonderful friends from one coast to the other; with one of my greatest loves the two years I spent in Los Angeles. It was party time and I soaked it up like a sponge. We worked very hard during the day and sometimes even into the night; and we played hard. Lots of good clean fun with some really wonderful people. The memories are as clear as if it happened yesterday and it was 40 years ago.

There have been many painful moments mixed in but, by the grace of God, I'm not able to dwell too long on unpleasantries.

The birth of my son, Robert, was certainly a highlight of my life. He is a beautiful young man married to Amanda and they have given me two precious grandchildren: Dakota Michael, 4 years old and Jolie Anne, 3 years old. I get to see them once a year whenever I can. My heart is saddened that they are so far away in Minneapolis.

Making the move to Florida in 1985 was a highlight moment in my life. And, as I stated in my story, when I found Jesus at San Isidro Catholic Church, I was ecstatic with joy. Jesus challenged me to grow, as He still does today. It seems when I feel like I'm doing everything according to His will, He allows a situation to happen that really tests my heart and lets me know there's still space for lots more growth.

Following the call to be a Poor Clare Sister has brought me such joy. It was hard at first saying good-bye to my son and so many precious friends. Our Lord cannot be outdone in generosity. He has sent so many dear and special friends since I came here 13 years ago. The love I have for our Lord deep within my being just grows and grows. I try at least once a day to give it away. So many do not really know that Jesus loves them and that they are special to Him! I have been blessed and loved; I am special to Jesus... just like you!